CULTURE SMART!
KENYA

Jane Barsby

·K·U·P·E·R·A·R·D·

ISBN 978 1 85733 858 4
This book is also available as an e-book: eISBN 978 1 85733 859 1

British Library Cataloguing in Publication Data
A CIP catalogue entry for this book is available from the British Library

First published in Great Britain
by Kuperard, an imprint of Bravo Ltd
59 Hutton Grove, London N12 8DS
Tel: +44 (0) 20 8446 2440   Fax: +44 (0) 20 8446 2441
www.culturesmart.co.uk
Inquiries: sales@kuperard.co.uk

Series Editor Geoffrey Chesler
Design Bobby Birchall

Printed in Malaysia

About the Author

JANE BARSBY is an English journalist, travel writer, and PR consultant who has lived in Kenya for more than twenty years. She has featured regularly in magazines such as *Travel Africa*, *Msafiri* (the in-flight magazine of Kenya Airways), and *Travel News and Leisure East Africa*, and is the author of a series of guidebooks on the Kenyan national parks and reserves. Formerly an international conference and exhibition organizer with experience in Africa, China, Russia, Europe, and America, Jane has organized numerous trade exhibitions and conferences in Kenya. She works extensively with the Kenyan hotel and tourism industry, and has also undertaken a number of commissions for the United Nations in Kenya and in Sudan.

The Culture Smart! series is continuing to expand.
For further information and latest titles visit
www.culturesmart.co.uk

The publishers would like to thank **CultureSmart!**Consulting for its help in researching and developing the concept for this series.

CultureSmart!Consulting creates tailor-made seminars and consultancy programs to meet a wide range of corporate, public-sector, and individual needs. Whether delivering courses on multicultural team building in the USA, preparing Chinese engineers for a posting in Europe, training call-center staff in India, or raising the awareness of police forces to the needs of diverse ethnic communities, it provides essential, practical, and powerful skills worldwide to an increasingly international workforce.

For details, visit www.culturesmartconsulting.com

CultureSmart!Consulting and **CultureSmart!** guides have both contributed to and featured regularly in the weekly travel program "Fast Track" on BBC World TV.

contents

contents

Map of Kenya

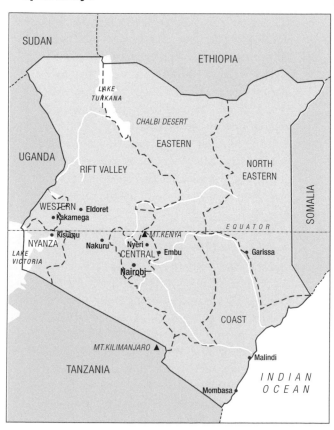

introduction

Known as the "Cradle of Mankind," the original
Garden of Eden, and the place where, six million
years ago, Millennium Man walked the Tugen
Hills, Kenya is the ethnic homeland of us all. It
was from Kenya's nurturing embrace that the
earliest humans wandered forth to colonize the
world. On the shores of Lake Turkana, however,
where *Homo erectus* took his first upright steps,
little has changed. The searing wind still scours the
waters of the "Jade Sea," hippos wallow alongside
crocodiles, and nomadic tribespeople live a life
essentially unchanged from that of their ancestors
fifty thousand years ago.

Kenya later became the adopted home of more
than seventy different groups of ethnic African
migrants, each with its own distinctive cultural
identy. It is a land of miraculously harmonious
contrasts: tropical ice, teeming wilderness, vibrant
culture, and gentle tolerance. A place where,
despite the burdens of poverty, drought, and
famine, the phrase *Hakuna matata* ("no problem")
embodies the national attitude, and a smile is the
most valuable currency.

Today fifty-six national parks and reserves
offer sanctuary to some of the world's most ancient
and most threatened creatures. The country
contains some of the last primordial rain forests
and boasts more species of birds than anywhere

else on earth. Stunningly scenic, steeped in history, a sportsman's paradise, and a lover's idyll, Kenya was in the past a playground for royalty, millionaires, aristocrats, and eccentrics, and still remains one of the world's most popular tourist destinations. It is not for the trappings of tourism, however, that it is usually remembered. Visitors come away indelibly touched by the warmth, sincerity, and generosity of the Kenyan people; and the poorer the person, the richer the welcome.

Culture Smart Kenya! is not intended as a travel guide. It won't tell you how to climb Mount Kenya or where to spot lions; but it will tell you how to make the most of your visit by interacting fully with the people. It describes many different aspects of Kenyan life, both private and public, from traditional African customs to modern business practices. By offering insights into people's behavior, values, and attitudes, it will prepare you for cultural differences and help you to respond with respect and understanding.

Karibu means "welcome" in Swahili, and is the usual answer to the question *Hodi?* which means "May I draw near?" Traditionally a visitor to an encampment would call this question from the darkness beyond the fire, and the answer would be returned: "Welcome, step into the light."

Key Facts

Official Name	The Republic of Kenya	Named after Mount Kenya, or *Kirinyaga*, "the Mountain of Whiteness"
Capital City	Nairobi (*Nyrobi*, meaning "Place of Cool Waters" in Maa)	Official population 3.9 million, unofficial population over 4.5 million
Main Cities	Mombasa is the coastal capital and the largest port on the East African coast.	The other major cities are Kisumu, Eldoret, and Nakuru.
Area	225,000 sq. miles (583,000 sq. km)	5,200 sq. miles (13,400 sq. km) is inland water (part of Lake Victoria). The coastline is 333 miles (536 km) long.
Borders	Kenya is bordered by Ethiopia, Sudan, Somalia, Uganda, and Tanzania.	
Climate	Varies with altitude and terrain. The low, tropical coast has an av. day temp. of 81–88°F (27–31°C), Nairobi 70–79°F (21–26°C).	Jul.–Aug. is winter. Jan.–Feb. is dry, Mar.–May wet, Jun.–Sept. dry, Oct.–Dec. wet.
Economy	Agriculture: 80% of the population, contributes 30% of GDP, and 50% of export earnings.	Tourism is the largest export earner. Industry contributes 19.5% of GDP.
Currency	Kenya shilling (KSh) KSh 99.62=US $1 (2016)	Coins: 50 cts, KSh 1, KSh 5, KSh 10, KSh 20, KSh 40 Notes: KSh 50, KSh 100, KSh 200, KSh 500, KSh 1, 000

Population	45,925,301 (2015 est.), 41.56% under 14; growth rate at 1.93% one of highest in world	Life expectancy at birth: 63.77 years. About 43.4% of population below poverty line
Ethnic Makeup	The two major language groups are Bantu and Nilotic. Largest tribes in Bantu group: Kikuyu, Meru, Gusii, Embu, Akamba, Luyha, Mijikenda; in the Nilotic group: Maasai, Turkana, Samburu, Pokot, Luo, Kalenjin. In the third, Cushitic-speaking, group: El-Molo, Somali, Rendille, Galla. The coastal region is home of the Swahili people.	
Religion	Christianity, Hinduism, Sikhism, Islam, and traditional beliefs	
Language	English (official), Kiswahili (national), multiple ethnic languages (Bantu, Cushitic, and Nilotic language groups)	Literacy: 87.4% of population over 15 can read and write.
Government	An independent republic with a democratically elected parliament	The President is the chief of state and head of government.
Electricity	220–240 volts, 50 Hz	Standard 13 amp, three square-prong plugs
Internet Domain	.ke	
Telephone	International telephone code: +254	To dial out of the country, dial 000 followed by required country code.
Time	GMT +3 all year round	Almost 12 hours of daylight. Sunrise and sunset 6:30 a.m. and 6:45 p.m., varying only by 30 minutes during the year

chapter one

LAND &
PEOPLE

GEOGRAPHY

Named after Mount Kenya, or *Kirinyaga* ("Mountain of Whiteness"), which lies almost in the center of the country, Kenya straddles the equator and covers an area of just under 225,000 sq. miles (583,000 sq. km). Bounded to the east by the Indian Ocean, it shares borders with Somalia, Ethiopia, Sudan, Uganda, and Tanzania. Most of the north and northeast of the country is either uninhabited or sparsely inhabited desert.

The Kenyan landscape is divided into two distinct halves: the eastern half slopes gently to the coral-backed seashore; the western portion rises more abruptly through a series of hills and plateaus to the Eastern Rift Valley, known in Kenya as the Central Rift. West of the Rift is a westward-sloping plateau, the lowest part of which is occupied by Lake Victoria. The highest point in the country is the snowcapped peak of Mount Kenya, at 17,000 ft (5,199 m) the second-highest mountain in Africa and one of the largest freestanding mountains in the world with a base diameter of 124 miles (200 km). The coastline extends some 333 miles (536 km) from the Tanzanian border in the southeast to the Somali border in the northeast. The main rivers are the Athi/ Galana and the Tana. The major lakes are Victoria,

Turkana, Baringo, Naivasha, Magadi, Jipe, Bogoria, Nakuru, and Elementeita.

CLIMATE

Kenya displays great contrasts in topography and climate: snowcapped peaks give way to deserts, palm-fringed beaches to rolling savannah plains, alpine highlands to the lunar semideserts of the northeast. Since the country lies on the equator, the climate remains stable all year. The days are sunny and hot, but the nights can be cool.

Broadly speaking, January to February is dry; March to May is wet ("long rains"); June to September is dry; October to December is wet ("short rains"). The coast is always hot with an average daytime temperature of 81–88°F (27–31°C). The average daytime temperature in Nairobi is 70–79°F (21–26°C), while the temperatures elsewhere depend on altitude. The period July to August marks the Kenyan winter.

FLORA AND FAUNA

Kenya's flora is diverse: along the coasts are forests containing palm, mangrove, teak, copal, and sandalwood trees. Forests of baobab, euphorbia, and acacia trees cover the lowlands to a height of around 3,000 ft (915 m) above sea level. Extensive tracts of savannah grassland, interspersed with groves of acacia and papyrus, characterize the terrain at heights from 3,000 to 9,000 ft (915 to 2,745 m). The principal species in the dense rain forest of the eastern and southeastern mountain slopes are camphor and bamboo. The alpine zone, above 11,600 ft (3,550 m), contains large plants of the *Senecio* and *Lobelia* genera.

Despite the tremendous losses inflicted by hunting and poaching during the twentieth century, Kenya teems with wildlife. There are eighty major animal species, ranging from the "Big Five" (elephant, buffalo, rhinoceros, lion, and leopard) down to tiny antelopes such as the dik-dik, which is slightly larger than a rabbit. At least thirty-two endemic species are endangered.

An ornithologist's paradise, Kenya is the finest country in Africa for bird-watching, boasting 1,137 species of birds and sixty IBAs (Important Bird Areas). It is common to spot more than one hundred bird species in a day.

Kenya's wildlife conservation area is 17,000 sq. miles (44,400 sq. km) or 7.6 percent of its total area. For national parks and reserves, see pages 119–21.

ENVIRONMENTAL CONCERNS

Deforestation is a major problem. With one of the highest population growth rates in the world, Kenya requires ever-increasing amounts of agricultural land for crops and firewood for fuel. However, some 10 million trees have been planted over the past two decades with the help of private groups and tree nursery programs. There is soil erosion and desertification in some areas. Significant water pollution has followed the increased use of pesticides and fertilizers, and contamination of supplies means that only about 50 percent of the rural population has access to safe drinking water.

CITIES

The capital, Nairobi, from the Maasai word *Nyrobi* meaning "Place of Cool Waters," also known as the "Green City in the Sun" and "Safari Capital of the World," has a population of around 3.9 million people (the unofficial figure is closer to 5 million). It came into being in May 1899 as a supply depot created by the European builders of the East African railway, located at "Mile 327" from the coast, high enough above sea

level to avoid the malaria mosquito. The largest city in East Africa, it is also one of the youngest, the most modern, the highest at 3,600 ft (1,700 m), and the fastest growing.

Other urban centers are Mombasa (the main port on the Indian Ocean), Kisumu on the shores of Lake Victoria, Eldoret, Thika, and Nakuru.

THE KENYAN PEOPLE

Kenya is a cultural microcosm of Africa. Groups from all over the continent have migrated there for centuries, each with its own distinctive cultural features. As a result, Kenya has more than seventy ethnic communities, speaking close to eighty different dialects; all are united under the striped green, black, and red national flag (green for the land, black for the people, and red for the blood spilled in the struggle for freedom). Unity is expressed in the national motto *Harambee*, which translates as "let's all pull together."

The Population

For many years Kenya enjoyed the dubious distinction of registering the highest population growth in the world. Then, at the turn of the millennium, the growth rate slowed down dramatically. The high-speed growth had stemmed from the fact that, until very recently, a man's social and economic status in Kenya was largely determined by the number of children he sired. And, since polygamy was also widely accepted, a man of consequence could boast of having fathered maybe a hundred children, often more. Kenyan tradition also dictates that, once married, a couple must name a child after each of their own parents; which means they must continue to produce children until they have two of each sex. Add to the above the fact that Kenyans universally adore children, and that most Kenyan women would not consider themselves fulfilled unless they had borne at least one child (whether married or not), and the reasons for the explosive birthrate are all too clear.

As to the sudden decline in the population growth rate, this has resulted not only from the impact of AIDS on Kenyan society, but also from the growing

realization, especially among the rural population,
that today's couples can neither support nor finance
the education of so many children. The emergence
of a Kenyan middle class has also affected the
growth rate, with many professionals choosing to
establish financial security before starting a family,
and then opting to have only as many children as
they can afford to educate to university level. The
changing social structure has also introduced a new
phenomenon, the professional, and often single,
Kenyan lady, who increasingly chooses either to
remain childless, or to have just one child.

Officially the population of Kenya is around
46 million, though the actual figure may be much
larger, and the forecast annual growth rate is
1.93 percent (2015 estimate), which reflects the
expected increased death rate due to AIDS—more
than 1.3 million Kenyans (5.3% of the adult
population) are infected with the HIV virus. Under-
fourteens account for 41.5 percent of the population.
Urban Kenyans, constituting 25.6 percent of the whole,
are concentrated in a few large cities such as Nairobi,
Mombasa, Kisumu, and Nakuru, while 67 percent
of the people live in rural areas, mostly in the high-
rainfall arable areas of the central highlands, and
Western Kenya. The north and east of the country,
80 percent of the land, contains only 20 percent of
the population.

LANGUAGE AND IDENTITY

As we have seen, more than eighty languages are
spoken in Kenya. English is the "official" language and
Swahili the "national" language; both are taught in

ETHNIC MIX

Kenya's ethnic or tribal mix (the word "tribe" is still used both officially and in casual conversation) is approximately:

Kikuyu 22%

Luhya 14%

Luo 13%

Kalenjin 12%

Kamba 12%

Kisii 11%

Meru 6%

Other nationalities 10%

ETHNICITY AND LANGUAGE

Bantu-speaking people

Luhya, Gusii, Kuria, Akamba, Kikuyu, Embu, Meru, Mbere, Tharaka

Coastal Bantu: Swahili, Mijikenda, Segeju, Pokomo, Taita, and Taveta

Nilotic-speaking people

Luo, Maasai and Samburu, Turkana, Teso, Njemps, Elmolo, Kalenjin, Marakwet, Pokot, Tugen, Kisigis, Elkony

Cushitic-speaking people

Boni, Somali, Rendille, Orma, Boran, Gabbra

Kenyan schools, Swahili at primary level, English at secondary level. Most Kenyans, however, speak at least three languages—English, Swahili, and their "tribal" or "mother" tongue. Some, who come from marriages of mixed ethnicity, speak more. In the rural areas, however, visitors may find that English is either only sketchily understood, or not at all. Broadly speaking,

Kikuyu, Luo, and English are the most widely used languages; "up country" Swahili is spoken in varying degrees of grammatical accuracy, and *safi* (pure Swahili) is spoken almost solely on the coast. Most of the tribal languages fall into one of two groups: Bantu and Nilotic.

What follows is a brief introduction to some of the major "tribes" that the visitor to Kenya is most likely to encounter.

The Maasai

The Maasai have long remained the ideal mental conceptualization of the Western European idea of an African "noble savage." Tall, elegant, handsome; walking with a gentle spring of the heel, seemingly proud and indifferent to all but the most necessary external influences.

(S. S. Sankan)

Perhaps the best known of Kenya's tribes, the Nilo-Hamitic Maasai are a nomadic people whose lifestyle has remained essentially unchanged for centuries. The daily rhythm of life revolves around the constant quest for water and grazing for their cattle. Thought to have migrated to Kenya from the lower valleys of the Nile, the Maasai are distinguished by their complex character, impeccable manners, impressive presence, and almost mystical love of their cattle. The latter is based on the Maasai belief that the sky god, Enkai, was once at one with the earth. When the earth and the sky were separated, however, Enkai was forced to send all the world's cattle into the safekeeping of the Maasai, where, as far as the Maasai are concerned, they have remained. Brave and ruthless warriors, the Maasai instilled terror in all who came up against them, especially the early explorers. "Take a thousand men," advised the famous explorer Henry Stanley

when speaking of the Maasai, "or write your will."

Today, cattle are still pivotal to Maasai life and "I hope your cattle are well" is the most common form of Maasai greeting. The milk and blood of their cattle continue to be the preferred diet of the Maasai, while the hides serve as mattresses, sandals, mats, and clothing. Cattle also act as marriage bonds, while a complex system of cattle-fines maintains social harmony. Visually stunning, the Maasai warrior with his swathe of scarlet *shuka* (blanket), beaded belt, dagger, intricately plaited hair, and one-legged stance remains the most enduring icon of Kenyan tourism. That said, many a modern Maasai dons a suit for

work but, come the weekend, and he'll be back in his beloved traditional dress.

> *After deep reflection on my people and culture,*
> *I have painfully come to accept that the Maasai*
> *must change to protect themselves, if not their*
> *culture. They must adapt to the realities of the*
> *modern world for the sake of their own survival.*
> *It is better to meet an enemy out in the open and*
> *to be prepared for him than for him to come upon*
> *you at home unawares.*
>
> (Tepilit Ole Saitoti, Maasai chief)

The Kikuyu

The largest of Kenya's tribes, the Kikuyu live in the area around Mount Kenya where, at the dawn of the colonial era, they came into violent conflict with the European settlers, to whom large tracts of Kikuyu homeland had been apportioned by the colonial government. Since the possession of land is one of the foundations of Kikuyu social, religious, and economic life, this conflict rapidly spiraled into war, and it was the Kikuyu's formation of a political association against the British that sparked the infamous Mau Mau uprising of the 1950s, which eventually led to Kenya winning its independence. As a result of their early involvement in the fight for freedom, the Kikuyu have always played a dominant role in Kenyan politics and commerce, their most famous politician being Kenya's first president, Jomo Kenyatta, who even today is referred to affectionately as "Mezee" (respected elder). Perhaps more successfully than any other Kenyan tribe, the Kikuyu have adapted to the challenges posed by Western culture and technology, and their role in modern day Kenyan business is significant. However, the rural Kikuyu, traditionally agriculturalists, continue to combine small-scale farming with the growing of cash crops such as tea, coffee, and pyrethrum.

"There is no rain that does not enrich someone."
(It's an ill wind that blows nobody any good.)

Kikuyu proverb

The Swahili or Shirazi Peoples

The most prominent of the coastal people, the Swahili are not a tribe but the product of centuries of intermarriage between indigenous Kenyans and incoming waves of Persian, Portuguese, and Omani conquerors. First, around the seventh century, came Arab traders from the Persian Gulf, who plied the Kenyan coast in their dhows and gradually integrated with the native population. In the sixteenth century the Portuguese arrived, and finally, in the eighteenth century, the sultans of Oman took over

as rulers; both these sets of colonizers intermarried with the locals, just as their predecessors had done. The result was a colorful mix of ethnicity and language, which came to be known as "Swahili," which translates literally as "of the coast." Although the majority of Kenya's coastal people are Muslims, their relaxed way of life is worlds away from the stricter Islamic practices of the Middle East. Enjoying a vibrant culture, they excel in literature, art, and architecture, while the Swahili craftsmen are famous for their beautiful triangular-sailed dhows. Swahili cuisine is a glorious mélange of culinary influences: exuberantly spiced, steeped in coconut, and cooked with fresh lime and coriander.

Ndovu wawili wakisongana, ziumiazo ni nyika.
(When two elephants jostle, what gets hurt is the grass!)

Swahili proverb

The Asian Community
The importance of Kenya's Asian community is due to the influence it has had on the economy. It is a common misconception that this community is descended solely from the 32,000 indentured laborers from Gujarat and Punjab imported by the British at the end of the nineteenth century to work as "coolies" on the Uganda Railway. In fact, there had been people of Indian descent living on the coast for hundreds of years befor then, as evidenced by the introduction of bananas and coconuts to the economy. Nevertheless, the majority

the present Asian population are descendants of the 6,000 workers who elected to stay in Kenya after the railway was completed. Hardworking, aggressive in business, and highly skilled, they soon established a burgeoning commercial community, which still controls most of the country's retail trade. Initially functioning very much as an economic "colony" of India, to which its members tended to send most of their earnings, the Asian community is still self-contained, nurturing its own rich and diverse culture while remaining largely impervious to African cultural influences. Officially referred to as "Asians" since the partitioning of India in 1947, the present community consists of four main groups: Hindus (numerically the largest), Muslims (second largest), Goans, and Sikhs.

The White Community

Though small in number, the white community in Kenya is important because of the effect it has had on the country's development and culture. Referred to by Kenyans as *Muzungu* (singular) or *Wazungu* (plural), a Swahili word that roughly translates as "European" but can also mean "something strange and startling," the whites are largely synonymous with the British settlers, who began arriving in Kenya after it was declared a British protectorate in 1895.

An eclectic mix of landless aristocrats, big-game hunters, and ex-servicemen, they rapidly acquired much of Kenya's best farming land. They also achieved notoriety thanks to the riotous lifestyle of a very small group of wealthy sybarites who settled in the "Happy Valley" area of central Kenya, and inspired the book (and later film) *White Mischief*.

Unlike the previous migrants, most of whom had intermingled with the local population, the British came with the intention of introducing cultural change, rather than participating in cultural exchange. Resourceful and industrious, they had a profound effect on the indigenous Kenyan culture. British dress, language, architecture, farming, manners, religion, and leisure pursuits were imposed, whether the Kenyan people liked it or not. Today the dwindling *Muzungu* community is a blend of third-generation "white Kenyans," temporary business folk, and members of international aid organizations, many of whom are actively engaged in preserving or celebrating Kenya's traditional cultural heritage. Approximately half of Kenya's white population lives in Nairobi, many of them in the select suburb of Karen, named after Karen Blixen, author of the famous novel (and later film) *Out of Africa*.

The Dispossessed
The breakup of many traditional communities caused by colonial policies, and subsequent attempts by the Kenyan government to draw the urban population into the economy, have led to the large-scale movement of people to the cities. Most arrive pennyless and find shelter in the overcrowded and unsanitary shantytowns that have sprung up around the business districts (60 percent of Nairobi's population live in the slums), where they have little hope of finding a steady job or reasonable pay. The result is chronic urban alienation, seen in the high incidence of drunkenness, theft, rape, and violence.

A BRIEF HISTORY

*Almost certainly our first apelike ancestors emerged
in Africa, and few places offer as rich a fossil record
as this region.*

(Dr. Maeve Leakey,
National Museum of Kenya)

Kenya's evolutionary record goes back 25 million
years to a time when the ancient plateau of Africa
was wrenched apart and forced upward in a series
of massive earth movements and volcanic eruptions,
which continued for millions of years. Later, the
continent split from north to south to form the vast
crack of the Great Rift Valley, stretching from Jordan
to Mozambique. Climatic changes, lasting millions
of years, caused the expansion and contraction of the
African habitat: initially, a wetter climate enabled the
forests to spread, while in subsequent drier periods the
forests shrank into isolated pockets, to be replaced by
savannah grasslands.

With the arrival of the savannah, the apes inhabiting
the fringes of the fast-vanishing forests were eventually
forced to descend from their arboreal homes and
emerge into the glare of the plains, where they learned
to hunt and become omnivorous. Over vast stretches
of history, these same apes evolved into our earliest
ancestor, the hominid ape man, who in turn evolved
into *Homo erectus* and, eventually, into *Homo sapiens*.

The Cradle of Mankind (6,500,000–50,000 BCE)

Kenyan prehistory dates back to the dawn of time
when *Homo erectus, Homo habilis*, and other species

of early mankind inhabited the area. The first conclusive evidence of humans came in the form of fossils, most of which were found by the Leakey family on the shores of Lake Turkana (Koobi Fora), and in the East African Rift Valley.

Early Settlers (50,000 BCE–500 CE)

From around 50,000 BCE, Kenya's early humans lived as hunter-gatherers, learning how to make tools, communicate, and use fire (remnant communities remain in the form of the Daholo, Boni, Sanye, and Ndorobo). From 2000 BCE, the native hunter-gatherers were joined by huge numbers of migrants: occasional hunter-gatherers themselves, they were also livestock herders and farmers who traveled to Kenya from all over the African continent. The earliest distinct migration was of Cushitic-speaking people from Ethiopia, then in the first few centuries CE came the Nilotic-speaking ancestors of the present-day Kalenjin people, and from the west and south came the Bantu speakers, forebears of today's Kikuyu, Gusii, Akamba, and Mijikenda peoples.

The Swahili Coast Develops (500–1498)

Arab and Persian migrants started to arrive from 500 CE onward and the Kenyan coast quickly developed as a vital trans-Indian Ocean mercantile link. Trade rapidly expanded into the African interior, where goods were exchanged for ivory and slaves.

Portuguese Rule (1498–1698)

The Portuguese navigator Vasco da Gama landed in Malindi in 1498, and the Portuguese subsequently ruled the coast for two centuries. Theirs was a reign of economic and religious oppression. In 1593 they built Mombasa's Fort Jesus as their military headquarters.

Omani Domination (1698–1837)

In 1696 the Omani sultans challenged Portuguese rule, and in 1698 Fort Jesus fell. The Swahili coast then came under the rule of Muscat until 1837, when the Omanis were finally defeated by the British and the Germans.

European Exploration of Kenya (1844–92)

In 1844, two German missionaries, Johann Ludwig Krapf and Johannes Rebmann, became the first Europeans to venture into the interior. They were followed by Richard Burton and John Speke, and Dr. David Livingstone and Henry Stanley, all of whom came to Kenya in search of the source of the Nile. Joseph Thomson broke into new territory in 1882; he inspired James Hannington, who discovered Lake Bogoria, and Count Samuel Teleki and Ludwig von Hohnel, who discovered Lake Rudolf (now Lake Turkana).

The Partition of East Africa (1856–91)

British interests in East Africa climaxed at the end of the European power struggle known as the

"Scramble for Africa." In 1885 construction began on the Mombasa to Uganda railway (completed in 1901), dubbed the "Lunatic Express" after a satirical poem by Henry Labouchere.

In 1895 Kenya was proclaimed the British East Africa Protectorate, and by 1896 the first British settlers had arrived. Schemes were then introduced allowing a varied (though mainly middle- to upper-class or ex-service) group of British colonists, and also Afrikaners, to buy land at advantageous rates.

The First World War

By 1916 the Europeans had appropriated most of Kenya's farming land, arousing discontent between Kenyans and the settlers. During the First World War, one in four of the 200,000 African soldiers and porters conscripted into the King's African Rifles died; those who returned were deeply affected by the experience. In 1920 the British East Africa Protectorate became the Kenya Colony. Political associations began to spring up and by 1921 there were numerous protests and rallies calling for an end to colonial rule.

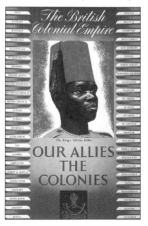

The Second Word War

During the Second World War the King's African Rifles fought bravely in Ethiopia and Burma. They returned to Kenya to find that land was being awarded to British soldiers in recognition of their services, but not to African soldiers; this greatly deepened the simmering resentment. Postwar African politics stepped up the pressure for independence with the formation of the Kenya African Union in 1946, headed by Jomo Kenyatta.

The Mau Mau Rebellion

Increasing tension culminated in the largely Kikuyu-led Mau Mau rebellion against British rule. In 1952 the British government declared a state of emergency and thousands of British troops were sent to Kenya. A fierce guerrilla war was fought and thousands of Kenyans were detained in concentration camps. The rebellion was finally quashed in 1956 with the capture of Dedan Kimathi, commander in chief of the Land and Freedom Army.

Independence, 1963

By 1960 the "wind of change" had begun to blow through Africa, causing Britain to relinquish colonialism. The Conservative government made the decision to pull out of Africa, and preparations 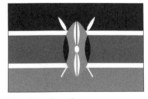 for Kenyan independence were made. On Madaraka Day—June 1, 1963— Jomo Kenyatta took office as Kenya's first prime minister and on December 12, 1964, Kenya became a republic. From then, Kenya was viewed as a model of stability and progress and, with the blossoming of a vibrant tourist industry, the country seemed set for a bright and positive future.

Death of "Mezee" Jomo Kenyatta

In 1978 "Mezee" ("Elder") Jomo Kenyatta died and there was a nationwide outpouring of grief. Kenya's vice president, Daniel Arap Moi, smoothly assumed

power and introduced a philosophy called "*Nyayo*" (Footsteps), which perpetuated Kenyatta's vision of "*Harambee*" (Let's all pull together).

Kenya had effectively been a one-party state since 1964, and was officially declared one in 1987 with the Kenya African National Union (KANU) at the helm. By the end of the 1980s the people had become disenchanted and demands for multiparty democracy began. It was not until 1991, however, that President Moi acceded to internal and external pressure and agreed to hold elections in 1992 and 1997. Both these elections were marred by violence and failed to dislodge the ruling KANU party.

In 2002 an opposition coalition—the National Alliance and the Rainbow Alliance—won a landslide victory over KANU and President Moi graciously conceded defeat. Mwai Kibaki was sworn in as president and the National and Rainbow Alliances were merged to form the National Rainbow Coalition (NARC). The people were euphoric, there was dancing in the streets, and it was thought that a new era in Kenyan politics had dawned. The NARC coalition splintered in 2005 over the constitutional review process. Government defectors joined with KANU to form a new opposition coalition, the Orange Democratic Movement (ODM), which defeated the government's draft constitution in a popular referendum in 2005.

The Election Crisis of 2007

The presidential elections of 2007 saw President Kibaki at the head of the newly created Party of National Unity (PNU) pitted against Raila Odinga of the ODM. Odinga had a strong lead in the early returns, but Kibaki was declared the final winner. Accusing the Electoral Commission of collusion with the PNU, Odinga called for a recount and his supporters held mass rallies. The brutal police response inflamed feelings further, bringing underlying tensions to the surface. Bloody interethnic violence broke out between Kibaki's Kikuyu and Odinga's Luo and Kalenjin supporters, and there was criminality in Mombasa and Nairobi. Almost a thousand people were killed and about 600,000 displaced in the upheaval, with each side accusing the other of ethnic cleansing and genocide.

The bloodshed finally came to an end in 2008 in an historic power-sharing agreement brokered by a group of eminent Africans led by former UN Secretary General Kofi Annan. Kibaki remained president, Odinga gained the new post of prime minister, and a coalition government with an equal number of ministers for the PNU and the ODM was formed. The accord included a broad reform agenda, the centerpiece of which was constitutional reform. In August 2010 a national referendum saw Kenyans adopt a new constitution.

The new constitution introduced additional checks and balances to executive power and significant devolution of power and resources to 47 newly created counties. It also eliminated the position of prime minister following the first presidential election under the new constitution, which occurred on March 4, 2013. Uhuru Kenyatta, the son of founding president Jomo Kenyatta, won the elections in the first round by a close margin and was sworn into office on April 9, 2013.

GOVERNMENT AND POLITICS

Kenya became a republic in 1964, with a president and cabinet. The president is elected for a five-year term as both head of state and head of government. Based on the British parliamentary model, there is a legislature (the national assembly) of 210 directly elected members, plus twelve members who are nominated by the president, plus the speaker and attorney general as ex officio members. Multiparty elections were first held in 1992. Following the violence of 2007, the amended constitution reduced the power of the president, delegated more power to local government, and created a Kenyan bill of rights.

The president and deputy president are directly elected on the same ballot by a qualified majority popular vote for a five-year term (eligible for a second term). As well as receiving an absolute majority popular vote, the presidential candidate must also win at

least 25 percent of the votes cast in each of more than half of the 47 counties to avoid a runoff. Kenya is divided into one area (Nairobi) and seven provinces: Central, Coast, Eastern, Northeastern, Nyanza, Rift Valley, and Western.

The Judiciary

The legal system is based on Kenyan statutory law, Kenyan and English common law, tribal law, and Islamic law. Despite attempts to reform the judiciary, allegations of corruption persist, and there is a general lack of faith in the system's ability to deliver prompt and unbiased justice (many cases take years to come to court and judgment is often hampered by repeated and lengthy appeals). In rural areas, basic justice, dispute mediation, and matters concerning land ownership are often dealt with initially by the office of the chief. In urban areas, mob justice continues to be common (see pages 54–5, 141).

THE ECONOMY

According to the Index of Economic Freedom, Kenya's gross domestic product was US $132.4 billion in 2016, equivalent to US $3,084 per head. The country usually spends more each year on imports than it earns from exports. Although Kenya's real GDP growth has averaged around 5 percent for the past several years, it remains among the low middle-income strata of countries. And, while Kenya has a fast-growing entrepreneurial middle class, her growth and poverty reduction remain hampered by corruption. Unemployment is high at around 40 percent.

Agriculture is the most important sector of the economy, accounting for 25 percent of GDP. It employs 80 percent of the population and accounts for around 50 percent of export earnings. Although only about 4 percent of the land is arable, Kenyan agriculture is highly diversified. Potatoes, coffee, tea, cotton, cereal grains, beans, and tobacco are grown in the highlands, which is the prime agricultural area, while sugarcane, corn, cassava, pineapples, sisal, cotton, and cashew nuts are grown on the coast and in the lowlands. Livestock breeding and dairy farming are also important, while commercial fishing mainly satisfies only the local market.

Kenya has one of East Africa's most diversified manufacturing sectors, including food processing, agricultural products, small-scale consumer goods, oil refining, aluminum, steel, lead, and cement, plus service industries such as commercial ship repair and tourism. Tourism provides the greatest source of foreign exchange earnings.

In response to the rising demand for electricity, Kenya continues to develop its hydroelectric and geothermal projects. At present hydroelectricity supplies 44 percent of electricity, while geothermal power and thermal power contribute 14 percent.

KENYA TODAY

The country has come a long way economically since independence. The regional hub for finance, trade, and travel in East Africa, it is the world's top exporter of roses and vies with Sri Lanka to be the second largest grower of tea after India. However, the economy is still dominated by agricultural and horticultural exports.

Economic development is also dependent on a mix of foreign aid, grants, and loans; it is hampered by the population being four times as large as it was forty years ago, resulting in ever-expanding towns, unwieldy bureaucracy, wages failing to keep up with inflation, and government controlled organizations resistant to change. There is a severe imbalance in income distribution: the richest 10 percent has 48 percent of income, the poorest 10 percent have 0.76 percent, while each year half a million school graduates compete for around 70,000 new jobs. As a result about half the population remains below the poverty line.

"*Jua Kali*" and "Self-Help"

The good news is that, despite its problems, Kenya has developed a flourishing informal economy, known as the "*Jua Kali*" sector. "*Jua Kali*" means "hot sun," and refers to the roadside artisans who run small businesses such as welding, mechanical work, woodwork, or plant nurseries. Another area of healthy growth is in the so-called "self-help" sector. This includes groups of women who get together to knit, sew, weave, do beadwork, or carry out other forms of traditional handicrafts. Not only do these groups generate income, they also provide a much-needed social support network for the women, who can profit from their businesses and pay for the education of their children.

Kenyan Tourism Back on Course

Tourism suffered badly during the 1980s and 1990s, the result of worsening security, banditry, poaching, ethnic clashes, reported human rights abuses, floods, drought, and terrorism. From the millennium onward circumstances began to change and the winning combination of beautiful scenery, national parks,

perfect climate, a long-established hotel and catering sector, and a charming and hospitable population eventually triumphed. After the crisis in 2007–2008 tourism plummeted, but it has since recovered. The income from one tourist is thought to support thirty jobs, and each job in tourism will probably go a long way to support an extended family of twenty to thirty people.

Multiparty Democracy—A Rocky Road
Politically the last two decades have seen a shift from a one-party state to a multiparty system; this has not, however, been accompanied by any significant improvement in government accountability or the rule of law. The good international reputation Kenya enjoyed in the 1960s and 1970s has been steadily eroded by underinvestment in infrastructure and repeated instances of corruption. It emerged from the events of 2007 with an historic settlement, however, and it enjoys good relations throughout the region.

Kenya provides shelter to approximately a quarter of a million refugees. It is a member of the United Nations, the Commonwealth of Nations, and the African Union.

VALUES & ATTITUDES

TRIBAL IDENTITY

For many Kenyans tribal ethnicity is the single most important part of their personal identity. Although the average Kenyan may outwardly have drifted away from tribal customs, the language he or she

speaks (their "mother tongue") is a mark of ethnic distinction. Many Kenyans also follow traditional practices, which manifest themselves in all kinds of ways, from the manner in which the festive roast goat is served to the names they give their children. Increasingly, the more contentious rituals, such as female genital mutilation, are largely outlawed, although circumcision still remains the main rite of passage for boys entering adulthood.

The advent of multiparty politics in 1992 promised to put an end to much of the political tribalism that was so prevalent during the eras of Kenyatta and Moi, who tended to favor their own tribes economically. As the election riots of 2007 showed, Kenyan politics is still divided along tribal lines and will probably remain so for a few generations yet. Socially, however, overt demonstrations of tribalism are increasingly frowned upon, and the now fashionable code of "Corporate Social Responsibility" (see page 143) insists that tribal links should have no bearing on the job market.

BLACK AND WHITE

Racial discrimination based on the color of one's skin is largely unknown. The average Kenyan is more than happy with the color of his skin and wouldn't want it otherwise. Many find the pinkness and ungainly gait of white people slightly amusing. To describe someone as "black" is usual in Kenya. Indeed you'll often hear people from, say, Western Kenya, being called "very black." This is purely descriptive and recognizes the fact that the people around Lake Victoria are much darker than, say, their Kikuyu neighbors.

"White" people are generally referred to as *Wazungu*, Asians (Indian and Pakistani) as *Wahindi*, and all other non-Kenyans as *Wageni* (guests), occasionally as "you people." Despite the history of British colonization, the Kenyan attitude toward the British is generally benevolent; they are viewed as dependable, and as having contributed positively to national development. Old wounds regarding colonialism and the Mau Mau rebellion are rarely opened.

"KENYA IS BEST"

Despite the fact that the country is home to seventy ethnic groups, the Kenyan sense of national identity is strong. Temporary residents are often asked, "How long have you stayed here?" (Kenyans tend to use the verb "stayed" rather than "lived.") If you've resided in Kenya for over two years, it is often suggested that you are "almost" Kenyan: this is a compliment. And, while many of the more affluent Kenyans send their children to school or university abroad, and the Kenyan diaspora is extensive, most Kenyans will tell you that, though they enjoy living abroad, they always yearn to be home.

NETWORKING

Kenyans place great emphasis on showing respect for their fellow man. Thus, upon meeting someone, it is customary to shake hands and to inquire after their health and the welfare of their family. This is not just politeness; it relates to the fact that many Kenyans are forced to find work far away from the place of their birth, and travel back "home" only once or twice a year. News of children, family, births, and deaths is, therefore, crucial. Also, it dates back to a time when the population was constantly on the move, and when up-to-date news was of prime importance.

HOSPITALITY

Kenya has welcomed incoming groups from the dawn of time, and the tradition of extending a welcome and providing hospitality is deeply ingrained in the national psyche. What's more, the Kenyans are really good at it. So, whether it is welcoming a visitor into a hotel, into their home, or into their business premises, they can be relied upon to do everything in their power to make them feel at home. And if the visitor "enjoys," the Kenyans are delighted.

SOCIABILITY

In this hugely gregarious society a lone Kenyan is unusual, the Western love of privacy and seclusion is anathema, and visitors or residents traveling or living alone are viewed with compassion, while energetic attempts will be made to absorb them into the family or social group. Historically living in small huts where space is tight and life of necessity intensely communal, the Kenyans are no respecters of "personal space." Lines, therefore, are generally cheerfully tight-packed and chatty; and until recently, when roped-off lanes were introduced in banks, it was not unusual to have several fellow customers interestedly peering over your shoulder to determine the nature of your transaction.

EVERYONE MUST HAVE THEIR SAY

A reflection of the values imbued in the traditional "*Baraza*" (a community meeting held in the shade of a tree, in which everyone is invited to have his or her say), Kenyans are great respecters of your right to speak. Consequently they are loath to talk over you, cut in, or otherwise muscle in on your right to a share of the floor. It works both ways: Kenyan speeches can be very long.

"SWAHILI TIME"

The Kenyan attitude to time is complex, but essentially patient and relaxed. Kenyans endure long journeys, tedious bureaucracy, lengthy lines, and long working hours without complaint. Their concept of punctuality is casual, to put it mildly— they themselves will often jokingly refer to BMT, "black man's time."

A partial reason for this lies in the fact that Kenyans operate both on the world time system and on their own traditional time system, "Swahili Time." "Swahili Time" runs from dawn to dusk to dawn, rather than midnight to midday to midnight. Thus 7:00 a.m. and 7:00 p.m. are both one o'clock, while midnight and midday are six o'clock (add or subtract six hours to work out "Swahili Time"). Much is also due to the fact that the rigors of everyday life have taught the Kenyans the all-important skill of being able to live for the moment, without indulging in too much introspection about what has gone before or what the future may bring.

FAITH IS CENTRAL

No matter what their religion may be, Kenyans are exceptionally devout. Going to church on Sunday is an exuberant event that is absolutely not to be missed. The

Bible (or the Koran) is the book of choice, knowledge of the scriptures is aspired to, praying is part of everyday life, amplified religious meetings are held in most public areas at lunchtime, religious icons and sacred tracts abound in the home, office, and vehicles, and most Kenyans are named after religious figures.

INDUSTRIOUSNESS AND THRIFT

The Kenyans have a strong work ethic, with good reason. Half the population lives below the poverty line, there is 40 percent unemployment, thousands of university graduates cannot find jobs, and, particularly in the tourism industry, one salary will often support an entire extended family. Additionally, there is no social security system and the heavy cost of education and health is borne by families. Money is hard to come by, and sparingly spent. What little there is, however, is willingly shared with those who need it; and attending and contributing toward social fund-raising events, large and small, are obligations that everyone accepts.

Allied to this is respect for the value of education, viewed as the all-important means to "make something of oneself." For this reason, it is not uncommon to find fully grown men and women eagerly joining a class of eight-year-olds: it's never too late to learn. Truancy is unknown.

ORDERLINESS

Despite the fact that many Kenyan towns may appear to Western eyes to be rambling, litter strewn, and disordered, within their homes the Kenyans love neatness and order. Furniture is usually presented in a traditional "four square" manner, chairs positioned at ergonomically effective angles are relentlessly straightened, upholstery is protected by hand-crocheted antimacassars, and curtains are rigorously knotted so that they don't "get in the way." Every rural Kenyan housewife aspires to own an ornate cupboard in which she can stow her stove, her crockery, and her household utensils, and the smart shops of urban Kenya abound with vast and ornate "wall units," on which to display everything from the TV to the family photos.

EATING AND SHARING

Eating and sharing food is very important to Kenyans, not least because food is often in short supply. An indication of how highly they value this is found in the colloquial expression for someone known to accept bribes: such a person is referred to as "eating," and by inference not sharing. Preferring to eat in the shade together, and if possible around a table, Kenyans view white people's habit of picnicking with amusement. Why pack up your food and take it to the middle of nowhere, when you could eat it at home?

Baffled by Western eating habits they may be, but your right to eat in private will usually be respected; should you have something left over, the gesture of sharing will be much appreciated.

WASTE NOT, WANT NOT

As their nation regularly faces drought and famine, you will rarely find a Kenyan wasting either food or water. Both are regarded with great respect. Conversely, until recently, Kenya's forests, the guardians of most of the water, were viewed as inexhaustible sources of fuel, timber, and (when cleared) land. This is an attitude that is fast changing, though some in positions of power continue to be accused of "land grabbing."

WATOTO

Kenyans love children (*watoto*), who are highly valued as a continuation of their lineage, and until recently subscribed to the view that "the more you have, the better." This view is fast disappearing, largely due to economic constraints. Kenyans find the Western concept of "deciding not to have children" largely incomprehensible, and women who cannot or will not have children are either pitied or (in the more primitive rural communities) ostracized.

Unlike in the developed world, Kenyan children are usually silent (it is unusual to hear a Kenyan baby cry), well behaved, deferential, and acquiescent to the wishes of their elders: "spoiled" Kenyan children just don't exist. They are also expected to contribute to the social group by acting as goatherds, collecting fuel, cooking, and doing any number of other chores. In return, the responsibility for their upbringing becomes the responsibility of the group and, in the absence of "mother," an army of elder siblings and "aunties" takes over.

THE POWER OF THE "BIG MAN"

Kenyans have a traditional reverence for the patriarch; the modern Kenyan man is very much the "king of his own castle" and must be obeyed in all things. The wishes of the father are universally respected and the grandfather is revered. Kenyan society is also still structured around the father figure of the chief, whose blessing is required for everything from political advancement to cutting down a tree. "Mezee" Jomo Kenyatta, the symbolic "father of the nation," remains universally honored, his descendants occupy positions of authority in all spheres of Kenyan life, and people still file past his tomb in central Nairobi. The incumbent president, President Uhuru Kenyatta (Jomo Kenyatta's son), also enjoys enormous status, commands absolute allegiance, and is frequently referred to obliquely as the "big man."

THE "*KALI MAMA*"

It is one of the conundrums of Kenyan society that although Kenyan women are immensely strong in character (often referred to as "*Kali mamas*" or "fierce ladies") and highly respected within the community, they still bow to the dictates of their menfolk. Most Kenyan men revere their mothers, have a healthy respect for their wives, and are well aware of the risks involved in cheating on them; but many still do. The majority of Kenyan women adhere to the traditional view that their husbands are to be obeyed; that if they stray it is due to the lures of other women, and it is their duty to entice them back into the marital fold with smiles, good food, and attention to their needs.

Most Kenyan employers are well aware of the efficiency, professionalism, and dedication that female workers bring to their posts, but sexual harassment remains a threat to those wishing to progress. And while most fashionable young Kenyan women think it's fine to wear body-hugging jeans or short skirts, in rural areas it is still possible for a mini-skirted woman to be stoned or stripped and thrown in the gutter for such a display of wantonness. But then, until very recently polygamy was normal (and is still not outlawed), selling your daughters to rich old men was one of the perks of fatherhood (and still is in the Maasai community), and "disciplining" your wife was considered necessary (domestic violence and the abuse of girl children is still a major problem within Kenyan society).

A SENSE OF STYLE

Kenyans are meticulous, stylish, and fashionable dressers. No matter how humble the home from which they exit, the suit will be pressed, the dress smart, the children faultlessly presented. In the rains, women carry their shoes to avoid them becoming spoiled; schoolchildren do likewise, and everyone clutches an umbrella. In general, Kenyan women

prefer to dress modestly; it is considered provocative to expose thighs and breasts, and office desks are fitted with "modesty panels" (to prevent covert views of a woman's legs). Conversely, many city girls wear impossibly tight jeans, clinging tops, and tottering heels; while their rural cousins stick to decorous skirts and blouses with a simple scarf tied around the hair. Weddings and other such events are an excuse for "putting on the style," and, if invited, you will compliment your hosts by dressing up.

At the coast, or in areas of Muslim culture, women are still veiled (the black coverall is known as a *bui bui*, which means "spider"), and the Asian community is fairly equally divided into those who

choose to wear traditional forms of dress, and those who don't. When in Mombasa, Malindi, and Lamu, visitors should respect Islamic customs and avoid skimpy clothes in public places. They should also bear in mind that topless sunbathing is illegal and will generally cause embarrassment.

Happiness is a New Hairdo
Kenyan women love having elaborate "braids"
woven into their hair (in salons, kiosks, or in their
backyards) and will happily spend hours having
their hair straightened, colored, and otherwise
altered: the results are stunning. Out in the bush,
the Maasai warriors spend similar amounts of time
braiding each other's hair, embellishing it with mud
and ocher, and ornaments ranging from buttons to
plastic roses.

THE HUNTER-GATHERER LEGACY
Fifty-thousand years ago all Kenyans were hunter-
gatherers. As we have seen, a few groups of hunter-
gatherer "bushmen-type" tribes still exist, but the
majority of Kenyans have metamorphosed into
nomadic herders, ranchers, farmers, entrepreneurs,
and the urban dwellers of the new millennium.
Some of the essential values of the hunter-gatherer,
however, can still be detected.

Meat-Eating
Hunting, though prohibited by law, and by the fact
that most of the ancient hunting grounds are now
national parks, still takes place; and the illegal trading
of "bush meat" (illegally hunted meat) remains
common. Modern-day Kenyans, meanwhile, retain
their love of meat eating, especially *nyama choma*,
which refers to any kind of meat roasted over coals.

Gathering and Exchange
The ancient legacy of "gathering" has survived in the
importance of bee-husbandry and honey gathering.

Maasai ceremonial life, for instance, is entirely dependent upon honey, and this delicious product is marketed by community cooperatives nationwide. Beer, the modern-day equivalent of "golden nectar," is an essential ingredient in Kenyan social life. The Kenyan love of barter dates back to a time when honey and forest products were exchanged for meat or other goods.

Survival of the Flexible
Characteristics of the hunter-gatherer live on in the Kenyan ability to survive adversity; also in the instinct for self-reliance, industriousness, thrift, and the acceptance of an essentially simple lifestyle. The traditional Kenyan respect for the equality of all members of the social group, their commitment to cooperation for the good of all, and the importance of family (and extended family) also point back to an earlier time. Most important of all, modern Kenyans retain their ancient ancestors' ability to adjust to change, imitate other material cultures, assume the dress and learn the languages of their global neighbors, and to do it so well that they rapidly become indistinguishable, but only when it suits them. Supremely adaptable and quick to learn, Kenyans have not only absorbed Western technology but have also bypassed much of the learning curve and jumped ahead, acquiring a discerning taste for Mercedes, cell phones, and all things micro.

"SOMETHING SMALL"
As a consequence of the intricate network of familial and tribal loyalty in Kenya, and also the traditional

idea that one favor always deserves another, the existence of corruption is accepted by the majority of Kenyans as "the way things are." Bribes are referred to as "*chai*" (tea) or "*kitu kidogo*" (something small) and range from a few shillings to the parking meter attendant, to the alleged millions exchanged in the major scandals of the day—which "go right up to the top," as the newspapers delight in reporting. The government acknowledges the problem of graft and is making strenuous efforts to clamp down on it. Thus in most government offices you will see notices against corruption and mailboxes inviting you to provide information on corrupt employees.

In general, visitors don't suffer from the effects of corruption as much as the Kenyan people themselves and it would be rare for a visitor to be openly asked for a bribe. How to react to such suggestions is very much dependent on the circumstances (joining the ranks of the "corrupt" may be preferable to spending eight hours in a Kenyan police cell, for instance). In general, the optimum response to a bribery suggestion is one of avoidance (see also page 153).

LIVING WITH POVERTY

A little under half of all Kenyans, we have seen, live below the poverty line, large numbers regularly go hungry, drought is a regular event, disease and disablement a cross that must be borne, beggars are an accepted feature of society (many are disabled, lepers, or homeless mothers with children), and glue-sniffing, rapacious street children are just part of normal life. In the cities, vast markets sell *mitumba* (secondhand clothes imported from the developed world); and the shopping for and wearing of *mitumba* is a favorite pastime among all levels of society. In the schools, meanwhile, it is not unknown for an entire class of forty-odd children to share one textbook.

Such poverty can come as a severe shock to visitors from the developed world, who tend to overcompensate by giving away money, sweets, pens, and clothes. However, according to Kenya's numerous charity organizations, this is not a good idea and merely promotes a degrading "begging mentality"; they suggest that it is better to give generously to recognized charities and help agencies. Many Kenyans, though, subscribe to the view that "there but for the grace of God go I" and give to beggars on a regular basis with a smile and a greeting. For the many Muslim Kenyans almsgiving is a religious requirement.

PATIENCE AND VOLATILITY

Kenyans are inherently patient and peace-loving (apart from the criminal element, that is); it takes a lot to make them rise up, riot, or otherwise display their displeasure with their leaders, and such incidences are rare. Like their fellows all over the world, however, Kenyan students are rebellious and often take to the streets to express their views. Usually this results in a few smashed traffic lights, a heavy police presence, and the temporary closure of the university. Kenyan degrees can, therefore, take a while to complete.

However, violence, in the form of mob punishment, can flare up in instances of street crime and also at the scene of serious car crashes, where it is normal for hundreds of bystanders to rush to the scene.

VIOLENCE AND CRIME

Most visitors reading the Kenyan newspapers will be horrified by the level of crime, much of it violent. Muggings, rape, armed hijackings, abductions, and break-ins are a daily event; most homes have barred windows, "rape gates" protect the bedrooms, "panic buttons" summon vans of private security "heavies," guard dogs prowl, and it is increasingly dangerous to go out at night.

Visitors are not the only ones to be horrified; the majority of Kenyans are too, and they accuse the police of not being up to the job. This may be true, not least because, many suggest, the police force is underfunded and corrupt itself (stories circulate of people calling the police and being asked to provide gas for the police car). Truer still is the fact that thousands of Kenyans face extreme poverty, and the gap between the "haves" and the "have nots" is becoming harder to close.

COPING WITH ILLNESS AND DEATH

A combination of low life expectancy, high child mortality, experience within extended families, the high incidence of HIV/AIDS, the ubiquity of a number of deadly diseases (particularly malaria), the expense of medical treatment, and the dearth of hospitals and doctors (in some provinces there is one doctor for 120,000 people) has inured the

Kenyans to illness and death. Illness happens, and is viewed as the will of God; death likewise.

The AIDS/HIV Crisis
The prevalence of HIV/AIDS in Kenyan adults was estimated to be at least 5.3 percent in 2014 (the real figure is thought to be much higher), 90 percent of Kenya's prostitutes are HIV positive, and the country

has around 1.4 million people living with HIV/AIDS. The government has undertaken vigorous promotion to alert people to the need for sexual protection and for awareness of HIV status. Despite this, significant numbers of Kenyan men continue to visit prostitutes, view promiscuity as the right of the "red-blooded male," and scorn the use of condoms. It is also true to say that many people continue to deny the reality of AIDS. At the funerals of AIDS victims, their families will often attribute their death to something else; and in the notices of deaths in the newspapers, the word AIDS is rarely mentioned.

PEOPLE AND ANIMALS
Kenyans and Wildlife
Kenya's population explosion has had a disastrous effect on its increasingly fragile ecology, and one outcome is the competition between humans and animals for dwindling land and resources. Considerable resentment exists among the rural population living around the national parks: first,

because they feel that the land should be theirs to cultivate; second, because they derive no benefits from the much-vaunted tourism revenue; and, third, because they must endure the hardships stemming from living in close proximity to wildlife—despite the fences, and especially during droughts, the animals break out of confinement, trample crops, and maim and kill people. Today, strenuous efforts are being made to resolve this conflict by diverting tourism revenue into the provision of wells, schools, and medical centers, and by finding positive ways in which the local population can earn money from the wildlife (by selling handicrafts or acting as guides).

Despite the fact that very low entrance fees are available to Kenyan citizens, relatively few visit the parks and reserves. The reasons are varied: they can see no point in spending money on entrance fees; they are not very interested in wild animals; they lack the transportation necessary to tour the parks; and they don't have the leisure time for such pursuits. The Kenya Wildlife Service has made great strides in changing this attitude by providing free bus tours, encouraging school visits, and generally promoting the national parks to the people. Among the middle classes, weekend or day trips to the parks have now become popular, and there is a growing interest in and respect for the parks and wildlife, much of it due to the increasing exposure to them of Kenyan schoolchildren.

Cultivating the *Shamba*
Ownership of land is of paramount importance to a Kenyan. No matter how modest, most Kenyans

have a *shamba*, small plot of cultivable land; most of them are gifted cultivators and diligent gardeners. A small number of domestic animals are often kept as well.

Domestic Animals
The Kenyan attitude toward domestic animals is complex. The Swahili word for "animal" is the same as the word for "meat," *nyama*, harking back to the old hunter-gatherer days. Conversely, the Maasai are known for their passionate love of their cattle, all of which they know by name. Most Kenyan small farmers keep a few cows, sheep, goats, and hens, which are their pride and joy. If there is a celebration to be held, a goat is often purchased, and more often than not the man of the house will slaughter it himself.

Many Kenyan households have a guard dog, which is viewed as a working animal, sleeps outside, and eats scraps. Rabies is a potent threat, so stray dogs are generally scared away (by throwing small stones at them), yet in most towns you'll see motley mongrels loping alongside the townsfolk, while in urban areas puppies are held out for sale in the traffic, and most rural boys herding animals have a faithful hound in tow. Donkeys abound in the central highlands, often pulling little carts and being urged on with a stick; and camels are to be found both in the far north and on the coast, where they are nearly always cared for by a doting Somali.

chapter three

RELIGIONS
& BELIEFS

Despite the strong influence of the "newer" religions, old beliefs die hard. Kenyan religion is therefore often a synthesis of ancient beliefs and more recent, though no less fervently held, faiths. This is less true in the cities, but in the rural areas a third of the population at least is thought to observe traditional practices such as ancestor worship, sacrifice, spells, curses, and the use of sacred *kayas*, or natural shrines. These often coexist seamlessly with modern religious beliefs.

TRADITIONAL BELIEFS

Kenya is steeped in myths and folklore. As in other parts of Africa, the human and the spirit worlds are inextricably bound together. People communicate with the gods through the medium of ancestors, deities, or local spirits. Beliefs and rituals are closely connected to the coming of the rains, upon which life depends. The Borana of northern Kenya, for instance, believe that "Water is the gift of Heaven, and grass the gift of Earth." God is most commonly manifested in the sun, moon, stars, clouds, thunder, lightning, and trees, particularly the wild fig tree. Mountains may be venerated: newborn children of the Meru are held up to face Mount Kenya for blessing, while, according to the Kikuyu, Ngai (God, also known as Mugai) resides on the top of Mount Kenya. The Kenya Wildlife Service still reports elderly Kikuyu men found wandering high on the snow-clad slopes in an attempt to get closer to Ngai.

The Maasai Legend of the Sun and Moon
Long ago the sun married the moon but one day they fought and the moon struck the sun on the head. Of course the sun hit back, and damaged the moon. When they had finished fighting, the sun was so ashamed of his battered face that he became so dazzlingly bright that humans could not regard him without half closing their eyes. The moon, however, was not in the least bit ashamed and anyone looking at her can clearly see that her mouth is cut and one of her eyes is missing.

(Adapted from *The Masai: Their Language and Folklore* by A. C. Hollis)

The Ancestors
Belief in the power of ancestors remains strong. The Luo, for instance, believe in ancestral ghosts, other tribes that their ancestors reincarnate as children within the family. Among the Nandi, when a child is born it receives a "spirit" name, which relates directly to its ancestors. And even in fast-moving urban Kenya couples are still expected to name their children after each of the grandparents. Finally, the fact that ancestors are thought to bring unity to the family lineage, and a direct link with other lineages, goes some way to explain the phenomenon of the Kenyan funeral. Many of these are huge events that last for days, cost fortunes, and hundreds of mourners attend.

Shamans, Soothsayers, and Herbal Medicine

Many of Kenya's indigenous religions center on
those who can intercede with the spiritual realm.
Such people exist in many guises, from the so-called
"witch doctor" or wizard (whose services are regularly
called upon to deal with matters ranging from illness
to curses) to soothsayers, diviners, and shamans.
Each has his or her own method of addressing the
physical and spiritual needs of the individual. Some
use sacred items, like talismans and carved deities;
others, natural objects such as earth, stones, and trees;
yet others, simple tools such as shoes, which they
"throw" to determine what action is required. Such
practitioners are often expert in herbal medicine.

Herbal medicine is highly regarded: not only
is it cheaper and more easily obtainable than
pharmaceuticals, but it is believed to be more effective
since it treats the ailment in a holistic manner.
According to the World Health Organization

80 percent of the rural population turn first to herbal doctors and remedies, before consulting a regular medical practitioner.

The Sacred *Kayas* of the Coast

Down on the south coast, in the wooded hills that lie behind the tourist strip, are the remnants of an ancient religion. The sacred *kayas* are clearings in the forests, adorned by offerings, carvings, and flowers. These magical sites were traditionally maintained by groups of male elders as centers of spiritual rejuvenation, ritual, burial, and prayer. They were also the source of the medicinal herbs, fruit, and forest products that were central to the existence of the coastal peoples. In more recent times a growing disregard for traditional values, coupled with a rising demand for land and timber, have placed the *kayas* under increasing threat. Fifty-two remain, of which some have been protected as national monuments, but many have been drastically reduced in size or sold.

Creation Stories

Each of Kenya's ethnic groups has its own version of how the world was created. One of the best known is the Kikuyu creation story, whose influence remains so strong that most Kenyan families name their girl children after Mumbi (the tribe's mythological creator) or one of her nine beautiful daughters, and most rural Kikuyus strive to build their houses with the door facing Mount Kenya (Jomo Kenyatta's book on Kenya's cultural heritage is named *Facing Mount Kenya*). In rural areas the sacred fig, or *mugumo*, trees can still be found with small offerings at the foot of their mighty trunks.

THE GIKUYU (KIKUYU) CREATION MYTH

In the fiery dawn of time, when the earth trembled in the throes of creation, a dense cloud of mist stood over the land as Mugai (Ngai), the divider of the universe, descended to earth. There, upon the snow-capped peaks of the mountain called Kirinyaga, he made a dwelling place as his seat of mystery.

Mugai beckoned Gikuyu, father of the Gikuyu, to the sacred mountain and said: "You shall carve your inheritance from this land, it shall belong to you and your children's children." And Gikuyu went to a grove of sacred fig trees where, resting in the shade, he found the most beautiful of women. He took her for his wife and named her Mumbi, the creator of the tribe.

Gikuyu and Mumbi built a home and had nine daughters. Their nine daughters matured into beautiful women. Their cheerful laughter was like the sweet chorus of birds and their milky teeth gleamed like white doves in flight. When they walked, the melody of the beads around their waists rose to the sky, deep, somber, and enchanting. But with every full moon, they felt the flow of the rising tide searing like glowing firewood in their wombs. They beseeched their parents: "For many seasons you have held and comforted us but now we wish to have homes of our own so that your names may be whispered from generation to generation." For many moons, Gikuyu and Mumbi searched their hearts. At last, in despair, Gikuyu fell upon his knees. Raising his face to Kirinyaga he called upon his creator to bless his daughters with husbands. Mugai heard him and commanded Gikuyu to make a sacrifice in the fig tree grove. Heeding the commandment Gikuyu sacrificed a lamb and a kid and lit a fire with nine burning sticks and said: "We have come to beseech you for rain, which sustains our children. Say now that the rain may fall." And out of the fire came nine flaming young men whose backs were firm and strong like the trunk of the sacred Mugumo tree and when he saw them Gikuyu gave thanks and welcomed them into the homestead. The nine handsome young men could not resist the beauty of Mumbi's daughters and asked for their hands in marriage. Gikuyu blessed the marriages and as each daughter built her own hut and had a family, the name of Mumbi prospered.

When Gikuyu and Mumbi passed away, each daughter called together all her descendants, forming one clan under her own name. These nine clans merged together in unity, kinship, and solidarity and were given the ancestral name of "The house of Mumbi." And to this day, when the Kikuyu call upon their creator, they turn their faces to the snow-clad mountain.

Superstitions

Every tribe in Kenya has its own superstitions, some better known than others. Bees circling the head means news, good or bad, within two days.

A dog or a cat crossing one's path is unlucky. Colors can be lucky or unlucky: black is considered a "cool" entity, and therefore welcome; red is a "hot" entity, and so is not propitious. Red is also associated with modern-day Kenyan funerals, when red ribbons are tied to all the vehicles in the procession.

Spellbound Soccer

The awe felt for the power of the "witch doctor" is reflected in the name of one the nation's best-known soccer teams, Gor Maiya, called after one of Western Kenya's most famous wizards. Gor Maiya lived high on a hill in the Lambwe Valley, now Ruma National Park, and his sorcery was so powerful that he could see all things and controlled the whole of Western Kenya. People came to him for good magic and bad, knowing that he could read minds, cast spells, bring rain, kill with a look, and shape-shift in an instant from man to dog, dog to bull. Husband to twenty-two wives, Gor Maiya died in 1920, and his many descendants still populate the region around Ruma National Park. As for the soccer team, they still visit his hill before important matches, hopeful that, even from beyond the grave, his formidable powers will score them goals.

CHRISTIANITY

Christianity is Kenya's dominant religion, reflecting its strong missionary heritage. Protestants make up 45 percent of the population, Roman Catholics 33 percent, and African Christian faiths 10 percent.

The many different Christian sects all have an African flavor. Church groups often wear colorful clothes and headgear; on Sundays they parade through the streets with banners and drums, dancing and singing.

Music, rhythm, dancing, singing, and rejoicing are central to Kenyan religion, which is far more passionate than in Europe. Most churches have a choir, which will nearly always appear in distinctive costume; most are excellent and the best are world-class. Attending church is not only a spiritual occasion; it is also a prime social event, a chance to catch up with family and friends, and for young people to meet up. Consequently, on Sunday just about everyone, from the president down, goes to church, dressed in their Sunday best, with their entire family.

All over the country small churches spring up, sometimes built from *mabati* (corrugated iron), sometimes in rough stone, and sometimes even starting in a tent until funds have been gathered by the local pastor and his, often tiny, flock. When asked why Kenyans feel the need for so many small churches, one pastor explained that it was because they "have so many problems" and are exposed to so many temptations, which lead to and stem from these problems, that they need a very close, one-on-one relationship with their pastor. He acts as a hands-on father figure, who works round the clock exhorting his flock to lead a better, Christian life.

ISLAM

Muslims represent 10 percent of the population. There are large communities on the coast and smaller groups in the Northeastern region. All Kenyan towns and cities have a mosque: many have several but one usually serves as the focal "Friday mosque." Most Muslims in Kenya belong to the Sunni branch of the faith, the remainder to the Shi'a, of which there are three primary sects: Ismailis, Ithnasheris, and Bhoras. Of these the Ismailis, followers of the Aga Khan, are the most influential, not least because the Aga Khan has business and philanthropic interests in Kenya.

Despite the impact of terrorism on Kenya, which has been profound, the population remains cohesive and antagonism against the local Muslim community is almost unknown. This is due to the fact that the majority of terrorist attacks in Kenya have been perpetrated by the Somali terrorist group al Shabaab (meaning "the young ones"), in direct reprisal for the presence of Kenyan peacekeeping troops in Somalia. Latterly great attempts have been made to improve security along the Somali border and within the country itself. There have been repeated calls for Kenya to withdraw her troops from Somalia in the interests of public safety. The government, however, remains resolute in refusing to bow to terrorist pressure.

ASIAN RELIGIOUS GROUPS

All the major religions of India are represented in Kenya: Hindus, Muslims, Sunnis, Sikhs, Zoroastrians, Jains, and many more. Most large towns have Hindu and Sikh temples, many of them of great architectural splendor and intricacy.

HOLIDAYS AND CELEBRATIONS

The following official holidays are often marked by church services, parades, and other festivities. If a public holiday falls on a Sunday, the following Monday is observed as a holiday.

New Year's Day January 1

Id ul Fitr February/March (dates vary): for the Islamic population, the country observes this three-day feast at the end of Ramadan. The first day is an official holiday for Muslims; celebrations on the following two days take place after working hours.

Maulidi, soon after Id ul Fitr, is a festival to mark the birth of Muhammad; it is held in Lamu and attracts pilgrims from all over Africa.

Easter March/April (dates vary)

Labor Day May 1

Madaraka (Self-Rule) Day June 1: the anniversary of self-government, achieved in 1963 (though not yet with full independence). It marks the birth of the Kenyan republic.

Mashujaa Day October 20: formerly known as Kenyatta Day, Heroes' Day collectively honors all those who have contributed to the struggle for Kenya's independence.

Jamhuri, or Independence Day December 12: the most important holiday of the year, Jamhuri commemorates Kenya's liberation from British rule in 1963. The day is celebrated nationwide, with the presidential speech delivered by local government leaders, but Nairobi plays host to the most impressive festivities. In addition to speeches by the president and other officials, there are parades, fireworks, and special dances are performed in public squares.

Christmas Day December 25

Boxing Day December 26: a legacy from British rule, it derives its name from the old British custom of putting tips and bonuses in small earthenware boxes for servants and tradespeople on the day after Christmas.

chapter four

MAKING FRIENDS

MEETING PEOPLE

Kenyans are gregarious, hospitable, and easy-going. Intensely curious, they also take pleasure in meeting visitors and finding out about their way of life. So making friends is hard not to do.

As to how to meet people, the opportunities are endless: visitors can take part in the activities organized by the Nairobi National Museums of Kenya, join one of the many choirs for which the country is renowned, make contact with one of the international cultural institutes, take out temporary membership at a golf club, join the "Hash House Harriers," who hold weekly runs in all the major towns, join a gym, sports, or social club, or an amateur theatrical group, volunteer help to a wide range of health or religiously associated groups, or consult the bulletin boards in the major shopping malls or supermarkets, all of which post details of classes, leisure activities, educational facilities, and forthcoming events.

Alternatively visitors can go along to the most popular local bar or *nyama choma* joint, easily spotted by the number of cars pulled up outside, and just mingle with the crowd.

Kenyans place great value on their friendships. City folk are also increasingly aware of the benefits of "networking," a concept ideally suited to the "extended family" mentality. There is, however, an unwritten rule underlying the Kenyan view of friendship: whatever you have is to be shared, in times of plenty and scarcity alike. So, if a friend asks you for help, monetary or otherwise, you're expected to provide it. And vice versa.

TIME IS ELASTIC

The Kenyans, we have seen, have a very relaxed attitude toward punctuality. Arranging to meet with Kenyan friends, therefore, can be frustrating. Arriving half an hour late is nothing at all. Not arriving at all is not unheard of. Neither should be taken personally: "things" happen. In general, Kenyans are tolerantly amused by the Western obsession with punctuality.

The Kenyan attitude toward loans and "borrowing" can also be disconcertingly relaxed. So, if you're going to lend anything, be prepared for the fact that it might take a while to be returned, since the borrower's finances are almost always stretched to the limit, and time is elastic.

BLACK FACES, WHITE FACES

White visitors may find that they are mistaken for another white person, to whom they can see no resemblance whatsoever. This is due to the often-voiced perception among Africans that "all white people look the same." They don't mean it literally, but it is easy for people to be confused; and exactly the same thing happens the other way around. On the other hand, Kenyans rarely forget a face, value their friendships with visitors, and will always come up and say "Hello! Remember me?" This can prove embarrassing for the visitor, who may have interacted with scores of Kenyans in a short space of time. The best way to deal with this is to smile, exchange greetings, and (if necessary) explain the predicament: such honesty is always appreciated.

SAFARIS, SUNDOWNERS, AND KENYA COWBOYS

Of the Kenyan population, only 1 percent is non-African, mostly Asian, European, and Arab. Many of the largely British white community live in the Nairobi suburb of Karen (once Karen Blixen's coffee farm) in large houses, usually with extensive grounds, and often with horses. They tend to keep to themselves socially but, should you be invited to Kenya by a British friend, you may find yourself enveloped in a social whirl: new faces are always welcome. Sociable and sports oriented, the British are regular visitors to the national parks, where "safaris" and "sundowners" (cocktails in scenic

locations) are popular. Many are
now second or third generation
residents, and large numbers are
officially "white Kenyans" (holders
of a Kenyan passport). A substantial
proportion send their children to
school in England, yet many of these
yearn to come "home" to Kenya, where they
are affectionately dubbed "Kenya cowboys" or
"Ken chicks" due to their love of the outdoor life
and adventurous natures.

RESPECT FOR KENYA
Kenya fought a bitter battle for its independence,
and holds both its flag and its national anthem in
high regard. In deference to the Kenyan flag, visitors
should stand when it is either raised or lowered, and
when the national anthem is played. Kenyans love
their country, and while they may criticize its faults
the visitor should not.

POLITICAL PUNDITRY
Kenyans love to discuss politics, hold vehement
political views, read the daily paper avidly, have their
ears glued to the radio, and know all the latest twists
and turns in the political saga. Political gossip is
popular, and rumors spread like wildfire. In general,
they are happy to discuss politics with visitors and
will cheerfully deplore the quarrelsome nature of their
politicians, the existence of widespread corruption, the
inability of the government to maintain the roads, and
so on. However, in order to be taken really seriously in

a political conversation, the visitor must know exactly what her or she is talking about: who is who, who's just sided with whom, and who's said what. It also helps to have a working knowledge of scandals past, present, and about to unfold. In the absence of such knowledge, best stick to friendly general discussion on the values and beliefs of differing cultures.

VISITORS AND THE LAW

Kenyans may despair of their own legal system, which can be long-winded and opaque, but those who flout the law can find themselves in hot water fast. It is, for instance, a criminal offense to tear up or deface a banknote, to urinate in a public place (a problem, since public facilities are hard to find), to hire a prostitute, to buy or take drugs, or to remove wildlife products from Kenya (for example, elephant, rhino, or sea turtle derivatives, or coral). In the event of difficulties visitors should remember that the judicial system is based on the British model, so bond or bail can be granted at the police's or magistrate's discretion and all cases must be brought before a court.

RETAINING SELF-CONTROL

Kenyans consider it gravely insulting to shout at anybody, even with words of praise. Reared according to the dictates of a strict hierarchy in which children are seen and not heard, and where deference toward elders and superiors is valued, they respect self-control and quiet but measured speech. Thus, losing one's temper (whatever the provocation), swearing, or using demeaning language will be viewed as a demonstration of poor upbringing and bad manners. Initially politely ignored, such displays of anger cause embarrassment to the average Kenyan—on the behalf of the person who is behaving badly.

BOY MEETS GIRL

Kenyan courtships are not quite so "in your face" as in the West. Until recently it was unusual to see couples holding hands on the street, while kissing in public still isn't done. Generally, Kenyan girls are modest in their dress and behavior, which is something their men expect of them. Female immodesty is disapproved of by both sexes. Lack of funds and amenities means that courting is often done on long evening strolls, and the boys can be seen transporting their girlfriends on the seat fitted over the back wheels of their bikes.

In the urban areas, however, all this is changing. The young, modern, affluent middle classes have cars, incomes, and often homes of their own. Meeting in bars is very popular, as is dining out, going to the movies, or "hanging out" in fashionable clubs. Valentine's Day has taken Kenya by storm and it is now the done thing to send an enormous, ornate card, a fluffy toy, or roses to the one you admire. That said, most Kenyan women aspire to marriage and the "bride price" (see page 93) must still be paid.

ROMANCE AND THE VISITOR

If you ask most Kenyan women about Kenyan men, they will laugh and tell you how "macho" they are, and how they themselves would like to meet a "nice" European or American man who will "treat them well." Relationships between Kenyan women and white men are common; between white women and Kenyan men slightly less so. Meeting members of the opposite sex is not difficult in Kenya (unless the women come from strict religious households). Workplaces and social venues are generally relaxed, introductions readily provided, and everyone loves to chat. There are also countless bars and cafés where conversations can easily be struck up. Flirtation can appear a little heavy-handed; it isn't intentional and should be viewed as an opportunity for hilarity and banter.

Remember, though, that in Kenya visitors are generally regarded as "rich," and while beautiful young Kenyan ladies may find overweight, red-in-the-face, sixty-plus white men attractive, and delight in their conversation, it could be that other factors are involved. The same could be said of the matronly white women who are regularly to be seen strolling the beaches hand in hand with gorgeous young Maasai warriors.

"Beach Boys"

Where wealthy foreigners disport themselves, scantily clad, on a public beach, rich pickings are to be had. Thus, on the commercial beaches tourists must run the gauntlet of hundreds of so-called "beach boys," who accost them with offers of shells, jewelry, boat rides, guided tours, snorkeling, carved elephants (always of "ebony" which is in reality stained hardwood), undying friendship, pen pals . . . and much more.

Often fluent in French, Italian, German, and English, these young men are generally friendly and polite, if a little pushy, and it is considered rude to ignore them completely. Nevertheless, conversation with them will usually result in some kind of financial demand, however circuitously couched (the very least of which is being persuaded to "swap" your sneakers for theirs in the spirit of friendship). Unless you feel able to deal with this, it is best to smile broadly, say *jambo* (hello), keep walking, and respond to questions with smiling tolerance. Alternatively, just smile and say you'd rather walk on the beach alone—if polite and honest, you will usually be respected.

Countless attempts have been made to rid the beaches of their "beach boys," but as soon as one group has been offered gainful employment elsewhere, another arrives to replace them. Also present on the beaches are resplendent Maasai warriors, who strut the sands in beaded and hennaed adornment, allegedly in search of ladies wishing to sample their legendary sexual prowess.

Same-Sex Relationships
Homosexual activity is illegal in Kenya. Attitudes are changing, but it is still the case that same-sex relationships are not generally approved of, or understood. (The view seems to be that homosexuality represents "non-African" behavior.) The Kenyans are, however, a relaxed and tolerant people who believe in "live and let live." In general, then, the maintenance of a considerate attitude and discretion is recommended.

EATING AND DRINKING WITH FRIENDS
Eating is another national pastime, and one that is taken seriously. When dining with friends it's best to save the conversation until after the serious business of eating is underway (see also page 100).

When entertaining friends or guests, it is as well to remember Kenyan tastes and habits. Large portions are *de rigueur*; Kenyans don't believe in eating what they don't like just to please you and will carefully leave what doesn't appeal; liberal sprinklings of salt or requests for ketchup are not intended to disparage your cooking; meat is preferred well done; regional European dishes such as spaghetti can cause confusion (lead by example); women may refuse wine and request soft drinks; and puddings (the sweeter the better) are always a runaway success; cheese, on the other hand, is not a great favorite.

In general the Muslim and Asian communities, and certain other groups, abstain from drinking, though in some cases the men may bend this rule in exclusively male company. Kenyans who do drink, however, do so with gusto and the sharing of a beer among males lies at the bedrock of Kenyan social behavior. Should you be invited to a nondrinking event, or into a nondrinking household, it would be grossly impolite to introduce alcohol to the premises or to request it.

INVITATIONS HOME

Kenyan hospitality is a joy, and can be humbling, since it is often the case that the less they have, the greater the desire of Kenyans to share. Much emphasis is put on the provision of food, drink, and all the comforts of home and family. If you are invited to a Kenyan home take a small gift such as chocolate (or anything sweet), or perhaps something from your own country. "Bringing a bottle" is not part of Kenyan culture.

Do not arrive earlier than the time stated, but rather half an hour later. Should you arrive early, you may find that preparations are not complete and, though you will be welcome, you will be left to wait while a flurry of (female) activity goes on behind closed doors. Upon arrival, note whether shoes are left outside the door: this is often the case and is in deference to the cleanliness of the home. If your host removes his or her shoes, or if other shoes are left outside the door, do likewise. Good manners are highly valued by Kenyans so, if in doubt as to etiquette, simply follow the lead of your host and your efforts will be appreciated.

Food will usually be offered immediately, but don't fill up on the samosas and crisps; these are just a prelude to much more—all of which you will be expected to enjoy. Drink may take the form of soft drinks or tea rather than alcohol.

BEING A WEDDING GUEST

Should you be invited to a wedding it is customary to RSVP and to bring a gift with you—wedding registries are starting to be fashionable in urban areas, but in general any household items will be appreciated, and you can ask a family member for advice. Arrive hungry, dressed in your best, and in the expectation of many hours of conversation, food, dance, and gaiety. In many communities there are separate events for men and women, some of which take place well in advance of the ceremony. All will be carefully detailed on the invitation. In general, events follow a set pattern. Visitors will be warmly welcomed and gently advised as to when it is their turn, for instance, to join the dancing.

PHOTOGRAPHY

Kenyans have a passion both for having their pictures taken and for taking other people's pictures. And the arrival of digital photography has intensified this because now they can see the results immediately. Nevertheless, it is courteous to ask people for permission to take their picture, particularly in rural areas where superstition still suggests that the camera is a stealer of souls. A token payment is expected, more as a form of polite appreciation than anything else.

SMOKING

Smoking is relatively common, though not among women. Cigarettes are cheap and of reasonable quality. Technically, since the passing of the Tobacco Control Act in 2007 and the Tobacco Control Regulation of 2014, it is an offense to smoke in public places in Kenya; practically, however, the lines are blurred. Smoking is allowed in "designated smoking areas" but it is not always clear where or whether such areas exist, and the ban has had little effect on Kenyans' smoking habits.

DRUGS

Though marijuana (*bhang* or *bang*) is widely cultivated, cheap, and frequently smoked in Kenya, it is illegal and attracts penalties of up to ten years for possession. *Miraa* (*qat*), a local herbal stimulant that predates coffee and is deeply rooted in the culture, is legal and widely available. Traditionally chewed by people in drought-prone areas, it suppresses hunger, promotes wakefulness, and is closely related to amphetamine. Grown on the hills around Meru, *miraa* is the red-green young bark of the shrub *Catha edulis*, which is washed, stripped with the teeth, and chewed. Marketed in bundles of a hundred sticks called "kilos," it comes in various qualities and loses potency within forty-eight hours of picking, which is why it is wrapped in banana leaves and transported at speed. Street stalls often display banana leaves to show they have it in stock.

chapter five

KENYANS AT HOME

THE KENYAN HOME

Kenyans are essentially home loving and hospitable.
Their houses come in all shapes and sizes, from the
low, square, mud-packed dwellings of the Maasai,
through the wattle and reed huts of the Luo, the
courtyard-shaped homes of the Swahili, the corrugated
iron (known as *mabati*) shacks of the urban slums, to
the apartments, maisonettes, and houses of the cities.
Interior décor ranges from simple wooden stools and
an open hearth to plush sofas, lavish curtains, and
spacious verandas.

Visitors will note that urban homes have bars
on the windows and doors, and that many have

security buttons (small switches on the walls), which when pushed summon the services of a security van packed with guards. Both are a reflection of the high incidence of crime in Kenya, itself a reflection more of the crippling level of poverty than of an inherent lawlessness in the Kenyan people.

DOMESTIC STAFF

Due to the dearth of employment opportunities, the high birthrate, and the long hours often worked by those with jobs, it is usual for most urban Kenyans to have a maid, often a very young girl, sometimes a family member, who is brought into town from the rural areas. She will be responsible for running the home, cooking the supper, and caring for the children. More affluent households may also have an *ayah*, who is responsible for caring for the children (but who may cook, iron, and clean as well), and an *askari*, who is essentially a security guard, and who may be shared among a number of houses in a compound. The upper

echelons of Kenyan society (and the middle class is growing fast) may also have a cook, a gardener, and a driver. This situation is replicated in Asian and white households. Most domestic staff "live in," that is, they are provided with "staff quarters," furniture, bedding, water, electricity, and so on, in addition to their wages, which are often very low (the minimum wage is approximately Ksh 5,500 per annum, but domestic pay often falls below this).

Many domestic staff come from "up country," particularly from Western Kenya, where they often own a small farm or *shamba*, which is run by their wife and where their children live. "Leave" and "travel allowance" is provided by employers to enable them to visit their families from time to time. Courteous, charming, hardworking, and hospitable by nature, the Kenyans are excellent staff members, both private and in the hotel industry.

The Finer Points

When staying in a Kenyan household it is considered polite to tip the staff upon your departure. One delicate matter: do not embarrass male domestic staff by asking them to undertake the laundering of feminine underwear.

Because of the scarcity of employment, and the closeness of family networks in which "looking after your own" comes first, you may also find, should you get chatting to staff, waiters, or drivers, that they will often ask if you can find a job for one of their relatives, or whether you would like to employ them yourself.

This is a tricky request, as it could provoke difficulties with their current employers. Best to say that you will bear it in mind and that should something come up, you will let them know.

MODES OF DRESS

Kenyans take great pride in their appearance and tend to be smartly dressed for work, elegantly dressed for formal occasions, and fashionably dressed to relax. Many of the clothes are made by the competent local tailors, whose small shops—known as kiosks and always equipped with a hefty manual Singer sewing machine—can be seen all over the country. Clothes are purchased from the secondhand, or *mitumba*, markets, found in all the cities, towns, and villages; much of the knitwear is hand-done, and lately the large supermarket chains such as Nakumat have begun to stock good selections of economical but stylish clothing.

Over the last ten years, it has become increasingly acceptable for women to wear pants and jeans (though both may be frowned upon in rural areas). Nairobi tends to be something of a law unto itself: the girls there wear skintight jeans, clinging tops, and elegant heels without attracting anything other than the normal kind of attention, and ultra-smart suits are the norm for both sexes. During the rainy seasons everyone clutches an umbrella and it is not unusual to see women wading through the puddles holding their shoes in their hands to protect them from damage.

In the rural areas many of the children go barefoot and you'll also see them quaintly dressed in hand-me-downs (from their siblings) many sizes too large. Frilly nylon party frocks are very popular with little girls, often patently "to be grown into" and usually with the sashes undone.

A curious aspect of Kenyan dressing (to outsiders) is the penchant for wearing thick woolly jumpers and fleeces when the temperature is soaring; and for dressing babies in knitted suits, bootees, and pompom hats when it's 104°F (40°C) in the shade. The Kenyan perception of cold, however, is necessarily very different from that of Westerners.

Kenya may not have an official national dress, but there are two very distinctive fashion icons: the *khanga* for women and the *kikoi* for men.

Khanga

Worn all over Kenya as a wraparound skirt, apron,

shawl, baby carrier, and general all-purpose garment, the *khanga* originates on the coast, where Swahili women traditionally wear two at once: one as a skirt, one as a veil. *Khangas* were introduced in the mid-nineteenth century when a group of Zanzibari women came up with the novel idea of turning printed kerchiefs into multipurpose fashion items. They bought them in lengths of six, cut them into two lengths of three, and finally sewed them together to make a handy 3 x 2 sheet dubbed the *leso*, which could be put to all manner of uses.

Like all good fashion trends, the *leso* was quick to catch on and the enterprising local shopkeepers commissioned specially designed pieces of cloth ready printed with six designs. Because the early designs had a border and a pattern of white spots on a dark background that resembled the plumage of the crested guinea fowl, and as this bird is famous for being very noisy, very sociable, and for running around in bright busy bands chattering all the while, the *leso* soon became the *khanga* (Swahili for guinea fowl). And so ready-made *khangas* were born.

Early in the twentieth century some Swahili proverbs were added to the *khanga* designs and it became the custom to present *khangas* as dual-purpose gifts and social message carriers, from husband to wife, friend to friend, or mother-in-law to daughter-in-law.

Khanga Proverbs

Kuleya mimba si kazi : kazi ni kuleya mwana.
(Getting pregnant isn't work! The work is to raise the child!)

Mtaka yote hukosa yote.
(One who wants all, usually loses all.)

Njia mwongo fupi.
(The way of the liar is short.)

Kikoi

Now a high fashion item that is exported all over the world, the *kikoi* is a rectangular piece of cloth, similar to the *khanga*, but longer and less decorated. Traditionally woven on a simple loom, *Kikois* are usually plain-colored in the middle and striped down the sides. On the coast Swahili men tend to wear them instead of trousers;

they also come in handy as beach wraps. "Up country" they are worn as an alternative to pajamas and dressing gowns: an easy and elegant wrap to laze around in during the evenings and on weekends.

LIFESTYLES AND ASPIRATIONS

So great is the diversity of ways of life and of ambitions in Kenya that it is difficult to generalize. The half of the population that lives in poverty lives very much "for today," concerned only with obtaining food and shelter. Once these necessities are assured, most Kenyans aspire to own land and to build a house—whether a simple corrugated iron construction, or a full-blown balconied mansion. In Maasai land, though, a woman usually aims first to own a cupboard, in which to store simple household items, then a "sofa set" (a two- or three-seater sofa and two armchairs) upon which her guests may sit; and thereafter schooling for her daughters (still thought unnecessary in some households).

In urban areas the "sofa set" is also seen as an aspirational item, swiftly followed by a television, while in rural areas a radio is treasured, often lovingly covered with a crocheted cloth to protect it from harm. A bicycle is highly prized by rural Kenyans and will be customized with mud-flaps and a padded saddle (though not necessarily lights). Higher up the social scale, a car will rate highly (most Maasai yearn for a Range Rover, most rural Kikuyu for a good pick-up truck); and when you've really "made it" in Kenya you have to have a Mercedes Benz— wealthy Kenyans are known as *Wabenzi*.

Many middle-class people also aspire to educate their children abroad.

Finally, until very recently everybody in Kenya dreamed of having a phone. Or, if they had one: to having a working phone (Kenyan landlines are notoriously fickle; affected by water, falling trees, and countless other mishaps). With the arrival of the cell phone, however, all that has changed and nowadays it seems that just about every Kenyan has one. And every Kenyan seems to be on it.

STANDARD OF LIVING

Most Kenyan lifestyles are harder than those of the developed world. People tend to rise early; many have an arduous and uncomfortable journey to and from work; many don't get home until late in the evening; and when they do there are spouses, children, and relatives to be cared for. Working hours are long and many Kenyans work on Saturday, usually until 2:00 p.m.

The population is one of the world's fastest growing; housing is in short supply, so rents are high and living space is often cramped. In rural areas furniture is often minimal (a bed, a couple of stools, a small table, maybe a cupboard), and a huge percentage of Kenyans live without electricity or interior plumbing. Kerosene is universally used for cooking and lighting, and much of the population has an exterior, and often communal, "long drop" toilet, while washing is done under a tap. Most Kenyan children wear secondhand clothes, play with handmade toys, expect to help with household chores, walk to school, and often have no shoes.

Recent years, however, have seen the emergence of a thriving middle-class, who live in pleasant maisonettes or apartments, or on brand-new housing estates; they may have dual incomes, a car or cars, go on annual vacations, send their children to private schools, and share all the aspirations of people in the developed world. This trend is fast accelerating, as seen in the housing boom in cities like Nairobi, where apartment complexes are mushrooming and where the advertising billboards promote imported liqueurs, lavish wedding gowns, state-of-the-art phones, fridge-freezers, and fast cars, rather than the household soap and cheap cooking fats that used to be the norm.

HARAMBEE

The concept of "*Harambee*" or "pulling together" was one of the key planks of the Kenyatta years, when, in the aftermath of colonial rule, emphasis was placed on the need for cooperation, unity, and self-help; especially in matters relating to health care and education. These days *Harambees* are called to finance all manner of things, from a medical operation to a university education and from a wedding to a funeral. Usually organized by a committee and graced by a "guest of honor," who is often a local politician or dignitary (whose contribution is expected to be substantial), a *Harambee* is an event that involves eating and drinking—alcohol is not usually provided; "sodas," roast meats, rice, and chapatis are—and, often, dancing.

Primarily, however, it is a working event, and raising money is the goal. Consequently, every trick in the book is employed to ensure that the guests put their hands in their pockets. There are raffles and auctions, and guests may be asked to pay for the choice of a dance tune, pay if they are wearing blue (or any other color for that matter), or pay for a red rose for each lady member of their party. If you accept an invitation to a *Harambee* you will be expected to show up and pay up.

MARRIAGE À LA MODE

Marriage is big business in Kenya. Every girl dreams of getting married, preferably with a large and lavish wedding ceremony to which the entire extended family is invited, from the youngest child to the most ancient grandma. Guest lists run into the hundreds and so complex are these events that they are usually planned by a "wedding committee," which orchestrates every detail, from the quantity of roast meats, chapatis, spiced rice, and assorted vegetables to be served, to the breakdown of "sodas" (Fanta against Sprite, Coke versus fruit juice . . .). Though the menfolk may expect

to indulge in a beer or two, and although wine may be served for the toasts, alcohol is not an integral part of a Kenyan wedding, many of which are entirely "dry" (particularly the Asian events). Food, needless to say, is central and this is not an event to which you should wear tight clothes: eating is expected of you.

"Come You Stay"

Because they are so costly, Kenyan weddings are often postponed for many years by couples, who may decide to live together and start a family while saving up for the grand occasion. Thus it is quite common to see relatively mature brides and grooms, accompanied by their own beautifully attired children, smiling for the camera on the big day. When a couple decide to live together in advance of matrimony, this is often termed a "come you stay" relationship, which is understood by everyone (though not always the man) to culminate eventually in a formal ceremony. In some cases there will be a traditional marriage agreement, which is formalized at a later date.

"Bride Price"

No matter how polished and sophisticated a Kenyan girl may be, she must still be "bought" from her family by the man who wishes to marry her. The "bride price" is established by her father in discussion with the father and brother of the groom. It is indicated in a number of ways: in urban areas it may be set in monetary terms and payable in installments; in rural areas it will almost always be set in cattle, twenty-five to thirty animals being the average "price" (one cow is generally accepted to equal ten goats or sheep). Obviously the payment represents a major investment for a young man, and his entire family and friends will be expected to deliberate over and contribute to it.

THE BLESSING OF CHILDREN

Our children are like the bright moon.
(In other words, children bring light into the home.)

Maasai proverb

Kenyans, we have seen, place great importance on having children, and are horrified by Western women who decide "not to have any." Women without children are regarded as barren and to be pitied. In rural areas they may even be divorced or biblically "cast off." So earnestly do Kenyan women yearn for children that they are often born out of wedlock—because the couple cannot afford a huge wedding, because the man has "run off," or increasingly because the woman has decided that although she wants children she doesn't want to surrender her independence to the strictures of marriage in a macho society. Kenyan men, meanwhile, usually pride themselves on their families and, particularly in rural communities, view children as indications of their wealth, power, and virility. Kenyan grandparents usually not only demand grandchildren, but also expect to have one of them named after them.

> *Symbolically the children belong to the same age group as their grandparents; the name given to the first male child is that of his paternal grandfather and at the time of birth it is announced that it is he who has come.*
>
> (Jomo Kenyatta, *Facing Mount Kenya*)

Prized, treasured, and adored though they are, Kenyan children still conform to the "seen and not heard" and "speak when spoken to" school of upbringing. Impeccably mannered, softly spoken, mostly silent, and wide-eyed, they regard their elders with respect; and bad behavior, whining, demanding, or complaining is not an option. In addition, because Kenyan families tend to be extensive, complicated, single parent, multiparent or, in the age of HIV, no-parent units, the children are often brought up by a mixture of mothers, grandmothers, second wives, neighbors, and friends. Thus they grow up addressing any caring adult as "Uncle" or "Auntie."

Kenyan children view childhood as a time for shouldering their responsibilities and learning the skills that will allow them to contribute to the community. Thus, small girls undertake numerous domestic chores and become "little mothers" to their younger siblings, while small boys are proud to take on the very serious task of herding the goats and sheep, or helping in the field. Acutely aware from an early age of the value of food, money, and possessions, Kenyan children appreciate everything they get; hand-me-down clothes are a way of life, shoes are often a luxury, school may be several hours' walk away, and plates are always eaten clean. Instilled with an independent spirit from

an early age, most Kenyan children find their own diversions, creating footballs from bundles of plastic and toy cars from homemade wheels and wire.

EDUCATION, PASSPORT TO A BETTER LIFE

Education, though not compulsory in Kenya, is universally viewed with great respect, and seen as a passport to a better future. Until recently education had to be paid for by parents; this placed a heavy burden upon them, particularly in rural areas, and in some cases not all the children in a family could be schooled. In certain cultures, particularly among the Maasai, it was considered unnecessary to educate female children, many of whom were destined for an early (at puberty) arranged marriage, often with an elder within the community. In 2002, however, the government, assisted by the international donor community, honored its election promise and committed to provide eight years of free primary education for all children. Thereafter fees must be paid for four years' secondary and four years' higher education respectively. This is referred to as the "8:4:4 System."

Though classes are usually large, and the schools housed in simple buildings with few, if any, teaching aids, the general level of education is good and

Kenya's literacy rate of 87.4 percent (2015 est.) is considerably higher than that of its neighbors. Most schools insist that their pupils wear a uniform, some of which are very colorful. Only the private schools (fee-paying throughout) provide school bus services, and the majority of Kenyan children walk to school—often over considerable distances.

The five public universities are the University of Nairobi and Kenyatta University, both in Nairobi; Egerton University in Nakuru; Moi University in Eldoret; and the Jomo Kenyatta University of Agriculture and Technology. Of the private universities, many are supported by religious groups from overseas.

THE KENYAN FUNERAL

Life expectancy is low (63.77 years) and infant mortality high (40 out of 1,000 live births, in 2015), so funerals are frequent events. Because many people live and work away from their ancestral home, which is often in a rural area, these also require transportation and organization.

You may therefore see a string of cars, trucks, and buses packed with people, red ribbons tied to the side-view mirrors to signify a funeral, perhaps headed by a vehicle with the casket lashed to the roof with ropes, swathed in black plastic to protect it from the rain.

These processions will often travel many miles to deliver the deceased to the ancestral home, where they are usually buried on the family land, their graves marked by a simple white cross and sometimes a picket fence. Because of the hot climate, burials tend to take place as soon as possible. The body is usually dressed in the finest clothes, shoes, and jewelry that the family can afford. In Western Kenya in particular, immense sums are spent on elegant grave clothes, elaborate caskets, and huge funeral feasts to which sometimes hundreds of guests are invited, and which can continue for days of drumming, dancing, lamenting, and eating. The costs can be crippling and loans and advances are sought to finance them, many taking lifetimes to repay. In many communities the lavishness of the ceremony reflects the prestige of both the deceased and the bereaved—and no cost is spared.

High-profile funerals may be used by politicians as opportunities for inflammatory speech-making, which can cause bad feeling. Also, because many of the older generation practiced polygamy, brawls can break out over which wife and family is to bury the deceased, and in which plot. It is not unknown for wrangles to go on for years before the body can be released from the mortuary, or the casket disinterred and relocated.

Most Asian funerals are cremations, which the white community also tends to prefer, often scattering the ashes over places of sentimental value or great beauty, such as the Great Rift Valley.

chapter six

TIME OUT

Hardworking the Kenyans may be, but they also value their leisure, the amount and quality of which varies according to whether they live in an urban or rural area. In the countryside the working day is long; traditionally people rise with the sun (7:00 a.m.) and go to bed soon after sunset (7:00 p.m.). Their diversions are few so "time out" tends to revolve around eating, family, neighbors, and gossip. Listening to the radio is very popular, and if there is a television in the village, it will often be available to all. Women often weave baskets or do other handicrafts (which they sell) in the evening; men tend to gather in the local *hoteli* (bar), *duka* (shop), or *kiosk* (a small shed selling basic items) for a drink (alcoholic or not) and a chat. Reading of the Bible is popular in any spare moment, and a visit to church on Sunday is a must. Most rural communities also feature a weekly market, to which everybody goes.

Social events are opportunities for the entire community to get together; funerals in particular are attended by hundreds, include much eating, drinking, and socializing, and go on for days. The rural villages often brew their own beer from millet or bananas, or make their own palm wine. Both rural and urban communities also brew a spirit known as *changaa*, which is highly intoxicating, illegal, and often lethal.

In the urban areas there are many more amenities to draw on: transportation, shops, street markets, bars, hotels, sports clubs, and sometimes movie theaters. That said, the use of leisure time usually follows a regular pattern. Many people work on Saturday morning, leaving Saturday afternoon for shopping and general domestic chores. Sunday morning is devoted to church, and only on Sunday afternoon is there time to visit friends and family. In general, the concept of an annual two-week vacation does not exist in Kenya, other than minimally among the urban middle and upper classes. Domestic staff in the major cities receive annual paid leave (around two weeks), which they use to go back "home" to the rural areas to visit their family. And, though a time of happiness and bonding, this "leave" is also a time for hard work (re-roofing the family house, tilling the fields, or planting and harvesting).

Those living in the countryside have to work year-round to keep the crops growing, the livestock fed, the children educated, food on the table, and kerosene in the lamps. Due to the impact of AIDS/HIV, low life expectancy, high infant mortality, and high birthrates, much of the Kenyan's "free" time is spent in attending the seemingly never-ending round of extended-family events: mostly birth celebrations, weddings, and funerals.

SERIOUS FOOD

Eating, we have seen, is taken very seriously indeed, as you would expect of a nation where famine is still a common occurrence. Polite conversation at mealtime is not a requirement and you'll often find a group of Kenyans eating in appreciative silence before getting round to chatting after the meal is over. Rising early and often traveling long distances to get to work, most people have a hearty breakfast. Nor do they subscribe to the Western habit of "missing lunch": lunch is a major meal of the day. As for supper, most Kenyans will eat early, first because they go to bed relatively early; and second because they are firm believers in the importance of the family, and regard mealtimes as family occasions. In the cities, however, long working

hours, traffic jams, and "meeting up for a drink" after work mean that many people don't get home until late, so the evening meal tends to be light.

Fast food is a concept that has translated well to Kenyan life. Busy Kenyans may often pick up a pizza from the fast-food outlet at the gas station, or grab a bag of fries, a hot sausage, or a hamburger from a street vendor, and eat them "on the run." Kenyan parties or family gatherings will often feature "bitings" (snacks), which may range from potato chips and peanuts to samosas and fried chicken legs.

Eating customs vary throughout the country. Among the Samburu of Northern Kenya, for example, warriors will not eat in the presence of women; elsewhere, men are often served first, and children often eat separately from adults. Traditional food is usually eaten with the right hand (the Swahili word for "right" is *kulia*, which means "to eat with"), while a knife and fork are usually used with Western cuisine.

Traditional Food

An acquired taste for the visitor, the traditional staple of Kenya is *ugali* (thick maize dough) or *uji* (porridge), made from yellow maize meal, millet, or sorghum flour.

Ugali is eaten with a stew of beans, goat, beef, lamb, chicken, or fish. Rice and chapati are also eaten, particularly on the coast.

The all-time winner as far as most Kenyans are concerned is the national dish of *nyama choma* (roasted meat). This carnivorous marathon features hunks of goat (the preferred

choice), beef, mutton, or (rarely) chicken served flanked by traditional clay pots of: *githeri,* a rich vegetable stew; *irio,* a Kikuyu dish made of creamed peas, maize, and potatoes; *ugali* (see above); or *sukuma wiki,* a spinach dish (cooked with onions, garlic, tomatoes, and coriander) whose name, roughly translated, means "to get you through to the end of the week."

Nyama Choma Know-How

A national obsession, *nyama choma* is, as its literal translation suggests, "burned animal," usually goat. Adored by all strata of society, it usually consists of a selection of prime cuts, purchased by weight, cooked in front of you over hot coals, and brought to your table where it is sliced into bite-sized pieces by your waiter. Traditionally served with vegetables, these days *nyama choma* often comes with fries and large amounts of ketchup or chili sauce. Highly flavored, preferably chewy, it is a dish for "real" men (and women) and not to be contemplated by those with vegetarian leanings.

For the Love of Goats . . .

Goat meat is a universal favorite and goats will be slaughtered (often at home by the man of the house) for all feast days, celebrations, and holidays. Traditionally the whole goat is roasted over a brazier of hot coals. Specific cuts are reserved for honored guests, others for men, women, young girls, and young men. Nothing is wasted: the blood and entrails are made into savory dishes, the head and hoofs boiled. The ultimate compliment when eating goat is to say that it is "very soft" or "very sweet."

. . . and Other Creatures

Beef, preferably with plenty of fat and usually *halal* (suitable for Muslims) is popular, as is chicken (known as *kuku*), and "up country" in Molo (a sheep-rearing area) lamb is prized. Game meat (crocodile, giraffe, impala, gazelle, and ostrich) is served in tourist restaurants, and sometimes as "bitings" with "sundowner" cocktails. On the coast, crab, crayfish, lobster, prawns, king fish, parrot fish, tuna, sailfish, and marlin make excellent choices, but it's worth checking that they're fresh—that is, just caught, and not what Kenyan salesmen sometimes term "fresh frozen," which means recently defrosted. Kenyan brown and rainbow trout (introduced from Scotland by the early settlers) can be caught in mountain streams and freshwater crayfish are a delicacy around Lake Naivasha.

Hot Snacks and Fast Food

Around the cities it is common to see street traders cooking maize cobs on a simple brazier, which are bought as a between-meal snack. Close to large factories and building sites makeshift kitchens spring up serving cheap bean stews with *ugali,* and fresh fruit. Kenyans have a very "sweet tooth" and will often heap two or three spoonfuls of sugar into their tea, which they like to drink with *mandazi* (triangular deep-fried sweet doughnuts), biscuits, or cakes. They also love fries, often making them a meal on their own (with plenty of ketchup or fiery chili sauce).

Kenyans are great fruit eaters; favorites are

bananas, pineapples, mangoes, oranges, and papayas (served with a wedge of fresh lime). Sweet potatoes and avocados are also popular.

Outside Influences

Kenya's cuisine has also been influenced by its immigrants. The Indians who built the railway made curry, chapatis, and samosas part of the staple diet; Arab and Persian traders created the traditional coastal Swahili cuisine, redolent of fresh ginger, spices, chilies, coconut cream, lime, and crushed tamarind seeds. The colonial British made "curry lunch" a traditional Sunday fixture, and also introduced the "full English breakfast" (bacon, eggs, sausages, mushrooms, tomatoes, kedgeree, fried potatoes, toast, and marmalade), popular in safari hotels and lodges.

Vegetarianism tends to be viewed as a decided oddity by the average Kenyan, who delights in eating meat. Not by many Asians, however, many of whom are such committed vegetarians that they do not like meat to be brought into their business premises or homes.

EATING OUT

The choice and quality of cuisine in Kenya is great. Most hotels serve an international menu, which is usually presented as a broad-choice buffet. There are also some truly excellent Indian restaurants, and a broad range of Thai, Chinese, Japanese, Italian, Lebanese, and Ethiopian.

The waiter should be addressed either as "waiter" or "steward." Summoning a waiter with a crooked finger or a beckoning movement is not considered polite; instead, imagine the waiter is on the end of a string and draw him or her to you with a gentle tugging motion. Always check the bill: mistakes are to be expected and it's your responsibility to spot them.

Avoiding Trouble

Visitors to Kenya often initially suffer from stomach complaints for the same reasons that travelers do the world over. To avoid this, take heed of the colonial adage "Only eat it if you can cook it, boil it, or peel it," and avoid food that has been left uncovered (on buffets, for instance). Regard water with great caution, particularly when it comes in the form of ice. Never drink the tap water; and if there's no alternative boil it—for two minutes at least.

KENYAN DRINKING HABITS

Kenyans love beer (which is actually more like lager); and there are bars everywhere, ranging from simple roadside shacks to five-star cocktail bars with waiters in bow ties. In Nairobi, bar fashions are fickle: one month the bar of the moment is a timber-built cowboy-style hangout, next month it's a roadside pull-off. Finding out which bar is "hot" is easy—just look for the number of cars pulled up outside. As for the beer, there is a bewildering selection of brands, headed up by the famous "Tusker," a lager named after the brother of a brewer who was killed in an elephant stampede in the 1920s. "White Cap" (named after Mount Kenya) is another brew much loved by the old school, while the relative newcomer "Castle" is the product of imported South African brewing technology and is rapidly gaining popularity.

Kenya also boasts its own wine, made from grapes grown on the shores of Lake Naivasha, and a wine made from papaya; both could best be termed interesting. In general, Kenyans are not great wine drinkers, often regarding it with a kind of uneasy reverence and claiming that they "don't know much about it" and are not sure "how to serve it." This is fast changing, however, and in the larger towns and cities ladies of the business community have developed a decided preference for chilled white wine.

Beer-Drinking Etiquette

You will be asked if you will "take" your beer cold or warm. Strange as it may seem to Western tastes, most Kenyans prefer it warm; some have even been known to refuse to drink it chilled. Beer bought in bars is usually served in bottles and it is very bad form (a criminal offense even) to leave the bar with the bottle— there is a deposit on it. Traditional male-bonding beer-drinking sessions often favor a system of buying a copious amount of beer and piling it on the table as a sign of brotherly affection. When all parties have drunk

TIPPING

Tipping is not common among Kenyans, but it has come to be expected from visitors. In restaurants you may like to "round up" the bill with a small gratuity if the service has been good.

In the tourist-oriented sector a service charge of 10 percent is usually added to the bill, plus 16 percent VAT and 2 percent catering levy. Most hotels have a staff box, and prefer that you make a contribution to this (the contents of which are shared among all the staff), rather than tipping a specific staff member.

Tipping of taxi drivers is not required, unless you have received extra-special service.

Most tourist guides and safari drivers will expect some kind of a tip, and most go to great lengths to ensure that you have a good safari. There are no guidelines as to how large such a tip should be, but it helps to bear in mind that many people in Kenya live on less than a dollar a day.

When staying as a guest in a Kenyan household, it is customary to tip the house staff, on the basis that they will have had to work harder than normal during your stay.

enough the remaining beers can be put back behind the bar for another day. Once solely the preserve of men, in the cities beer drinking in bars is now socially acceptable for women.

Local Brews

Kenyans are also very fond of brewing their own *pombe*, which is a fermentation of either bananas or millet. Strong, frothy, and unusual in taste, it should be regarded with caution by the visitor. *Chang'aa*, an infinitely more vicious brew, should be avoided at all costs since it can, and often does, kill those who partake. Brewed up secretly and often consumed communally by large groups of locals, *chang'aa* contains levels of methyl alcohol that can result in blindness or death. Those who survive tend to stagger, weave about, shout at cars, be incapable of focusing, and smell strongly. Not surprisingly *chang'aa* is illegal and jail sentences of up to ten years are handed out for possession.

Caution: *Dawa* is the Swahili word for medicine; it is also the name of a cocktail that is typically served in tourist restaurants and is made with neat vodka, honey, and lemon juice. It goes down very easily and is extremely strong.

Nonalcoholic Drinks

Large numbers of Kenyans don't drink—for religious or social reasons. Inordinately fond of sweet, sugary concoctions, the nondrinking fraternity tends to favor "sodas," any form of fizzy drink such as Coke, Fanta, and something known as "stony" or, more properly, "stony tangawizi," which is ginger beer. Failing that, there are plenty of fresh fruit juices to choose from (passion fruit, mango, and orange being the favorites).

Every Time is Tea Time
Kenyans love *chai* (tea), which they drink all day long; it's also interesting to note that the word *chai* also means a tip or bribe. Originally native to China, tea was first grown in Kenya in 1903, but did not become economically viable until twenty years later. Now it is one of the country's major exports and is grown in vast

swathes of bright green, largely around the town of Kericho, which is the "tea capital" of Kenya.

Visitors to Kenya should be wary when ordering tea or accepting it in a home or office situation, since the Kenyan concept of *chai* is very different from the British (or even the American) one. Traditionally tea leaves will be boiled up with milk in a teapot and served piping hot, very milky, and very sweet (one way around this is to order black tea, which plenty of Kenyans also drink). Order tea in a restaurant and you'll get a pot of tepid water with a tea bag floating in it and a jug of hot milk. If you want good old-fashioned "British" tea, best to ask for "tea, very hot, please, with *cold* milk."

The Coffee Conundrum

Kenya may grow some of the finest Arabica coffee in the world, but until recently it was virtually impossible to get a decent cup of coffee there, even in the coffee-growing areas. Maybe this was because coffee is brewed with less than boiling water and poor quality beans in calcium-lined coffeepots. It is also often served stewed and reheated. The coffee revolution, however, has finally hit Kenya and there are now a number of chains serving world-class coffee in all its many forms.

Elsewhere, however, unless you're in a good hotel, you may be served a lukewarm, thick, black brew with a slight slick on the top, often accompanied by a jug of warm long-life milk. In business circles you will often find that if you accept the offer of coffee you will be presented with a flask of hot water, a flask of hot milk, and a can of instant coffee.

In contrast, on the coast you can sample the powerful Arabic coffee, poured from triangular brass pots into tiny china cups, and often flavored with cardamom.

MUSIC

Music is an important strand in Kenya's cultural weave, and has always played a major role in social and ceremonial life. Based on strong drumming, it usually incorporates communal dance rhythms (ankle percussion instruments are often used), powerful humming, chanting, and singing; traditional instruments

include flutes, lyres, and guitars. One of the oldest musical traditions, the *ngoma*, was originally a drum-related dance; now the word has come to mean any party or celebration. Modern Kenyan music has evolved through early Afro-jazz, African hip-hop, reggae, and rap to arrive at today's totally eclectic mix, heavily influenced by trends from the Congo, Zaire, Mali, and Tanzania. On the coast, the traditional Arab/Islamic *taarab* music features strongly, played by a full Arabic orchestra (mandolin, guitar, harmonium, organ, lute, and violins), and often featuring soulful lyrics.

For the visitor, countless opportunities exist to experience the Kenyan music scene: most hotels and tourism venues have music and dance on their entertainment schedules; many clubs and bars feature live performances; every Kenyan wedding or social celebration includes music (often very loud); radios tinkle all over the country (often held to the ear as people walk along); there are numerous music shops and market stalls offering a bewilderingly broad range of African music; and countless street traders offer tapes, CDs, and DVDs (many of them pirated) direct to your car window. The younger generation is as music mad as its forebears, only this time they've got the latest technology to play it on. Meanwhile, no visitor to Kenya will escape without hearing (and preferably singing along with) Kenya's unofficial national anthem, *Jambo Bwana*.

Singing

An integral part of both music and dance, the love of singing is deeply embedded in the Kenyan psyche. Communal singing (sometimes divided into male and female choirs) remains a major part of all tribal and social ceremonies, and provides the emotional bedrock of Christian church services. Kenya has some of the finest unaccompanied choirs in the world. Becoming a member of a corporate or community choir (all of which have their own costumes) is very popular, and a blend of whistling and singing whiles away the hours for

many a cow herder, housemaid, cyclist, or walker, all of whom can be heard unselfconsciously trilling their favorite song, often at the tops of their voices. On the social scene live singing performances are very well received, karaoke has made quite a hit, and generally, if you feel like getting up and grabbing the mike—go ahead.

Dancing

With music, dance is part of the foundation of Kenyan culture. Every region has its own particular form, and

every ceremony has its own specific dance. Among
the best-known dancers are the Maasai and Samburu
(famous for their effortless leaping), and, on the coast,
the Giriama (renowned for their hypnotic swaying).
Most tourist hotels showcase dance displays nightly
and participation by the visitor is always invited, and
difficult to refuse. Usually the dancers come from the
local community and perform their own tribal dances.
There are also a number of contemporary dance
troupes performing in Nairobi and Mombasa. As for
the average Kenyan, he or she loves to dance and any
opportunity will do. Discos abound on the coast and
in Nairobi and Mombasa, many clubs and night spots
offer a dance floor, and dance features strongly in all
the major social events, such as weddings, *Harambees*,
parties, and religious gatherings.

THEATER AND CINEMA

Nairobi has its own National Theatre, which hosts a
broad range of performances from beauty pageants to
dance displays. A few small amateur theater groups

also exist in Nairobi and Mombasa, while many small clubs will host comedians or one-man shows. Theatrical performances are very popular with schoolchildren and most of the major schools stage annual performances, particularly at Christmas, when there is a Kenyan version of the traditional British pantomime.

In recent years the Kenyan cinema scene has been transformed by the arrival, primarily in Nairobi and Mombasa, of a series of state-of-the-art movie theaters showing the latest Hollywood (and Bollywood) hits. Going to the cinema is now a highly rated urban pastime. In the rural areas no such luxuries exist, but from time to time a touring cinema van will arrive, set up a big screen, and invite the whole village to come and watch. There is a local homegrown filmmaking industry, still very much in its infancy, but Kenya has regularly featured as a backdrop to such global blockbusters as *Out of Africa* and *The Constant Gardener*.

SPORTS

Soccer is a national pastime and the national team, known colloquially as the Harambee Stars, and the big teams of the Kenyan Premier League (AFC Leopards, and Mathare United) draw massive crowds. And, while the grounds and pitches may not be up to the standards of the developed world, the action, passion, and enthusiasm certainly are. Kenyans also have an obsession with the English Premier League (most people favor Arsenal, Manchester United, or Liverpool), and you will see supporting slogans, flags, and paraphernalia bedecking trucks, *matatus* (minivans), bicycles, and bodies alike.

Running

Kenyan middle- and long-distance runners are among the world's best and it is the ambition of just about every child in Western Kenya to become world-famous as one of these. Kenya's runners are also beginning to dominate the world marathon events. This is remarkable when you consider that Kenya won its first Olympic gold medal in athletics just thirty years ago.

Much competitive running takes place abroad, but major urban centers have a weekly gathering of the Hash House Harriers, and Kenyan military, police, or professional runners training along city roads are a regular sight.

Golf

Golf is a favorite pastime of the business community, who use it as an opportunity for networking. For the visitor, playing golf in Kenya can be a novel experience. It is the only country to have the following rule: "If a ball comes to rest . . . close to a hippopotamus or crocodile, another ball may be

Kalenjin Gold

Most of Kenya's top long-distance runners are from one tribe, the Kalenjin. Over the past decade Kalenjin runners have won thirty-one Olympic and world championship medals, including twelve gold medals. Kalenjin men also hold world records in five of the eight distances between 1,500 and 10,000 meters. The success of the Kalenjin seems to lie in their having lived for centuries at altitudes of over 6,500 ft (2,000 m); they have developed an incredible capacity to increase their aerobic efficiency.

dropped at a safe distance, but no nearer the hole, without a penalty."

Kenya has more than forty golf clubs, mostly around Nairobi (including an eighteen-hole international standard course at the Windsor Golf and Country Club), Naivasha, Thika, Nanyuki and Nyeri, Kisumu, and Kitali. There are also some fine courses on the coast. In addition, the Muthaiga Golf Club plays host each year to the Kenya Open Golf Championship, which is a stepping-stone to the European PGA circuit.

Tennis, Squash, and Table Tennis

Visitors will find traditional Kenyan hospitality extended at any Kenyan sports club or international hotel. They will also risk being soundly beaten, since Kenyans excel at these sports.

Riding, Racing, and Polo

Kenyans are natural riders (many young boys in the rural areas grow up riding young steers), and Kenyan *sysces* (grooms) are renowned for their skills. For the visitor, Kenya offers excellent riding safaris (horse, donkey, and camel), there is an active equestrian/ polo community in Nairobi, and for those who enjoy the "sport of kings" the Ngong Road Race Course in Nairobi offers an eight-race card almost every Sunday afternoon with bookmakers and betting facilities.

Fishing
On the coast, in the mountain streams, and in the many lakes, fishing has been practiced since the dawn of time. Often equipped with simple spears or rods and lines, local Kenyan fishermen supply the tables of the nation with most of their fish. For the visitor, meanwhile, there is plenty to choose from: fly-fishing in the mountain streams, which were stocked with trout by the colonials; some of the world's best deepwater offshore fishing (marlin, sailfish, shark, swordfish, tuna, and wahoo); and lake fishing on Lakes Baringo, Naivasha, Turkana, and Victoria.

Diving
Kenya has some of the best dive sites and dive schools in the world, the coastal waters are warm all year round, visibility is excellent, wet suits are not required, and the Kenyan barrier reef ensures shark-free waters.

Driving
Kenyans are fast, enthusiastic, and, some would say, reckless drivers. Driving and car ownership are very popular. Not surprisingly then, the annual three-day East African Safari rally is a popular event. A rugged 1,900-mile (3000-km) rally, which has been held annually since 1953, it hurtles along public roadways

through Kenya, Uganda, and Tanzania and attracts an international collection of drivers. There is also the Rhino Charge rally in the Rift Valley—a ten-hour suicidal spin across tough unmarked terrain to raise money for rhino conservation.

ACTION AND ADVENTURE

Hang gliding, paragliding, micro-light flying, ballooning, and parachuting are all available. The choice of ocean watersports is world-class, and there is white-water rafting on both the Tana and Athi rivers. Kenya is also one of the most economic and pleasurable places in which to acquire a pilot's license.

Opportunities for climbing are many and varied but by far the most charismatic climb is still Mount Kenya, Africa's second-highest mountain. The challenges of climbing are combined with a good opportunity to make friends, both with the Kenyan guides and with the other climbers.

Kenya is one of the world's most popular bird-watching destinations, with over 1,300 species recorded. In Africa, only Zaire has more. There are also thousands of local enthusiasts.

SHOPPING

Kenyans love to shop. In rural areas the shopping will mostly be for food and provisions, and will be done by women. In urban areas, large shopping malls have appeared, offering not only supermarkets but also coffee shops, fast-food outlets, cinemas, children's playgrounds, day care, fashion stores, home decor stores, pet stores, book stores, toy stores, beauty salons, banks, and more. Consequently a trip to the local mall is a favorite weekend pursuit for families and singles alike.

For the visitor, the many handicraft outlets that dot the country may be of more interest. The choice of purchases is wide: carvings, baskets, woven sisal, handwoven wool rugs, handwoven garments, knitwear, beadwork, handblown glass, metalware, beeswax candles, essential oils, leather goods, soapstone, paintings, batik, tribal masks, spears, jewelry, home décor . . . Many of the items are produced by women's cooperatives or self-help groups, so your purchase will help them achieve such benefits as an income stream, education for their children, the ability to start a small business, or financial independence. When shopping for crafts in Kenya it is important to remember that bargaining over the price is expected of you.

The Art of Bargaining
Most craft traders are loath to give you a price.
They prefer to ask you what you will pay for an item.
If pressed, the price they open with will often be
unrealistically high; especially if you are white. One
way to circumvent this is to ask for the trader's "best
price," which may cut some of the wilder figures. There
is, however, a "real" price, below which the trader will
not go. Your job is to find this price. Methods differ.
You can take the offered price, halve it, and bargain up
from there. Or you can make an offer of a price that you
feel happy with, and bargain from there. The acid test is
walking away. If the trader lets you walk, your offer really
was unacceptable. If he or she calls after you—there is
still room for negotiation.

PLACES TO GO
National Parks and Reserves
Kenya's national parks and reserves rank as some of the
finest in the world. They are administered by the Kenya
Wildlife Service (KWS) as sanctuaries where human
habitation is prohibited and where wildlife can roam
free. Kenya's total wildlife conservation area is 17,100 sq.
miles (44,400 sq. km) or 7.6 percent of the country's total
area. The main national parks are Aberdare, Amboseli,
Hell's Gate, Lake Nakuru, Meru, Mount Elgon, Mount
Kenya, Nairobi, and Tsavo East and Tsavo. One of the
most popular tourist destinations, the Maasai Mara,
is designated a National Reserve. There are two major
marine parks: Mombasa Marine National Park and
Malindi/Watamu National Park. Details on all these can
be obtained from the Kenya Wildlife Service (KWS) on
tourism@kws.org or www.kws.org.

The difference between a park and a reserve is that a park allows no human habitation or grazing of domestic livestock and a reserve does. Reserves are also usually owned and run by a county council, whereas a park is usually owned by the state.

Once the great hunting grounds of Kenya's earliest inhabitants, the national parks and reserves are now areas of wilderness conservation that attract nearly a million tourists a year. As we have seen, to the local people, however, they represent a mixed blessing: their existence reduces the available agricultural land and prevents such age-old pursuits as hunting, collecting timber, and gathering medicinal herbs. There is also the so-called "human versus wildlife conflict"—despite the fact that most are fenced, wild animals still manage to break out into the local community in search of food, particularly during droughts. This results in damage to farms and, often, injury or death to the inhabitants.

In an attempt to diffuse the acrimony and redress the economic and social balance, both the Kenya Wildlife Service and a broad array of private game sanctuaries try to ensure that local communities benefit practically from the national parks and reserves (see pages 56–7).

Nairobi National Park

The world's only major national park located adjacent to a capital city, Nairobi National Park lies just five minutes' drive from the city center, offers a fine chance of spotting a rhino, and is extremely popular with the Nairobi locals, who take advantage of it for family outings, and to escape from the hustle and bustle. the park also offers the Safari Walk, restaurant facilities, and the Animal Orphanage. It is accessible in a two-wheel drive rented vehicle or by any city center taxi and is open daily from 6:00 a.m. to 7:00 p.m.

Safari Etiquette

Kenya has been the uncontested "Safari Capital of the World" since the first decades of the twentieth century, when royalty, aristocracy, politicians, and movie stars flocked here to hunt the plentiful big game. The word *safari* actually means "to travel" and can refer to any journey or trip. When in either a park or reserve visitors should observe the Safari Codes (see overleaf).

The Great Wildebeest Migration

Between early July and September each year the Maasai Mara is home to one of the greatest spectacles of the natural world. The great wildebeest migration involves some two million wildebeest and around half a million zebras (accompanied by many thousands of gazelle) trekking north from the adjoining Serengeti National Park in Tanzania in search of fresh grazing. Following close behind are lions, leopards, cheetahs, hyenas, and vultures. The crossing of the Mara River at full flood is the greatest test.

THE SAFARI CODE

- Respect the privacy of the wildlife—this is their habitat.
- Beware of the animals—they are wild and can be unpredictable.
- Don't crowd the animals or make sudden noises or movements.
- Don't feed the animals—it upsets their diet and leads to dependence on humans.
- Keep quiet—noise disturbs the wildlife and may antagonize your fellow visitors.
- Stay in your vehicle at all times, except at designated picnic or walking areas.
- Keep below the maximum speed limit (25mph/40kmph).
- Never drive off-road—this severely damages the habitat.
- When viewing wildlife keep to a minimum distance of 20 m (70 ft) and pull to the side of the  road to allow others to pass.
- Leave no litter and never light fires or discard burning objects.
- Respect the cultural heritage of Kenya—never take pictures of the local people or their habitat without asking their permission, respect the cultural traditions of Kenya, and always dress with decorum.
- Observe the rules—leave the park by dusk; never drive at night in a national park.

THE FIVE-STAR SAFARI CODE

In addition to the Safari Code, a few further rules set the safari aficionado apart from the tourist.

- If your driver is driving too fast or too dangerously ask him or her to slow down.
- View responsibly—tourist buses chase after wildlife, and it's not uncommon to see twenty of them surrounding one bemused lion. This is irresponsible and can seriously affect the animal's eating patterns. If more than two vehicles are at a sighting, don't join them. Wait until they have gone.
- An informed safari is an enhanced safari—carry guidebooks (about the park, wildlife, birds, and flora) and binoculars.
- Always travel with plenty of water, wear sensible shoes in case you have to walk, carry a hat, sunscreen, and sunglasses.
- It makes sense to wear khaki or green clothing, but multiple pockets and hunters' hats can look contrived.
- Strong scents scare animals, so strong-smelling toiletries are not a good idea.
- It gets chilly in the evenings so take a light fleece.
- On a walking safari never walk in front of the gun and pay rapt attention to the instructions of your guide. In the face of danger from wildlife keep still; don't run.
- Watch where you are putting your feet; though most of Kenya's 126 species of snakes are not venomous—some are.
- Do not walk in the long grass; never walk without shoes. Watch out for ticks, which can

transmit tick typhus to humans. Tuck socks
into shoes and pants into socks, and in areas of
"pepper" (very small) ticks spray clothing with
insect repellent before walking in the bush.

- When in tented camps, bear in mind that
  the walls are made of canvas, and that sound
  carries.
- Don't be a safari bore—few fellow guests will be
  interested in the details of your day's viewing.
- When tipping the guide (which is optional),
  bear in mind that many people in Kenya live
  on less than a dollar a day.
- Do not remove anything from a national park
  or reserve (this also applies to marine parks).
- Never get between a hippo and the water—stay
  well away from lake shores at night: hippos
  are very dangerous; more people are killed by
  hippos in Kenya than by any other animal.
- Be wary of baboons—they can and do attack
  tourists (usually for food); they can also open
  tents and climb in through car windows.
- Most freshwater lakes in Kenya harbor
  bilharzia-transmitting snails. These parasites
  can enter the body and seriously affect the
  immune system, so don't swim in lakes, rivers,
  or streams.
- The best time to view wildlife is very early
  (dawn) and from 4:00 p.m. to dusk.
- Avoid altitude sickness—before climbing or
  trekking above 9,800 ft (3,000 m) spend a
  couple of days near that altitude and have a full
  day's rest for each 3,300 ft (1,000 m) ascended.

Historical Sites

Kenya has more than four
hundred historical sites
ranging from prehistoric
fossil sources and petrified
forests to fourteenth-century
slave-trading settlements,
Islamic ruins, and sixteenth-
century Portuguese forts.

Kenya's World
Heritage sites are **Fort
Jesus** (sixteenth-century
Portuguese fort), **Gedi
Ruins** (thirteenth-century
Swahili town), **Koobi Fora** (three-million-year-old
palaeontological site), **Lamu** (sixteenth-century
Swahili port), **Mount Kenya** (the country's highest
mountain), **Hell's Gate National Park** (geothermal
area), and the **Maasai Mara National Reserve** (scene
of the annual migration of the wildebeest).

chapter seven

TRAVEL, HEALTH, & SAFETY

ARRIVING

The first thing you notice upon arrival in Kenya is the smell. If it has been raining, this is of parched earth made wet; if it is dry there's a blast of warm wind off miles and miles of savannah (or, as the local white community puts it, "MMBA—Miles and Miles of Bloody Africa"). You become addicted to both smells, symptoms of "getting the Africa bug"—falling in love with Africa.

The airline hub of the East African region, Kenya is served by two of the largest, most modern, and most efficient international airports in Africa. Jomo Kenyatta International Airport (JKIA) is half an hour's drive from Nairobi's city center, while Mombasa's Moi International Airport is even closer to the town center. Most tourist hotels have their own minibuses to transport guests, while a public bus serves both the Jomo Kenyatta and Moi airports.

Both JKIA and Moi airports are ultramodern, well run, and welcoming. Immigration formalities are swift, and if you need a visa, you can purchase one on the spot (US $50). Once outside you will be greeted by a sea of eager taxi drivers; if you want a cab, bear in mind that the driver should show you a tariff sheet and agree upon the price of the journey before

you begin. Kenyan taxi drivers usually welcome the opportunity of a chat. Good conversational gambits for the visitor include "Which part of Kenya do you come from?" and "Have you had any rain lately?" Kenyan politics (impenetrable to most visitors) is also a popular topic.

Depending on the time of your arrival, you will either drive straight into downtown traffic— both cities are plagued by major traffic jams—or sweep into town in darkness when the roads are less crowded. Depending on how recently the city council has repaired the roads, you may or may not encounter the famous Kenyan potholes, which can make for a bone-rattling journey. Upon arrival at your accommodation the decision whether to tip the driver or not, is yours—in Kenya it is by no means the custom (10 percent will be fine).)

GETTING ABOUT
Internal Air Travel
Domestic flights are a convenient and relatively affordable means of travel. They also minimize

the time spent on the roads, which are generally in poor condition and contribute to hazardous driving conditions. It is also well worth seeing this diverse and beautiful country from the the air. Frequent scheduled and charter flights operate from Nairobi's Wilson Airport and from Mombasa and Malindi to the main towns and national parks.

Trains

Kenya's single-track railway line, which runs from Mombasa to Kisumu (via Nairobi)—formerly known as the "Lunatic Express" for the simple reason that no one could quite fathom why, or indeed how, the British colonial government built it (see page 30)—is a railway enthusiast's dream. That said, it is worth remembering that it was completed in 1901 and has been seriously underfunded ever since, which has resulted in a number of serious derailments. The overnight service from Nairobi to the coast, however, is still regarded as one of the "great train journeys of the world" and should not be missed. Traveling at the leisurely pace of 35 mph (55 kmph), the overnight trains are timed

to leave the major stations of Mombasa, Nairobi, and Kisumu at about sunset and to arrive at their destinations just after sunrise. Choice of the "deluxe" option is recommended and allows for the hire of crisp, clean bedding and the use of relatively luxurious private sleeping compartments. Washroom facilities are not en suite but per carriage. Plans exist for the running of the railways to be concessioned to a private consortium but progress has been dogged by dissent and allegations of corruption.

Matatus

More a part of Kenyan culture than a means of transportation, the *matatu* is the means by which nearly all Kenyans, and a number of budget tourists, travel. Usually taking the form of minivans (sometimes converted station wagons), they ply specific routes, either within the cities or between the towns. Operated privately, *matatus* used to be luridly painted, covered in slogans and flashing lights, pounding out deafening rap music and driven at death-defying speeds by aggressive young men, the result of which was one of the highest road death rates in the world. Recently subject to rigorous regulations by the government (including engine-speed regulators, yellow stripes down the side bearing the route number and destination, seat belts, regulation number of seats, and uniforms for the ticket collectors, known as "touts"), the *matatu* has now officially grown up and is nowhere near as dangerous as it used to be. Which isn't saying much, since the *matatu* drivers still whiz along as fast and aggressively as the roads permit. Typical *matatu*-driving behavior features constant honking; hurtling down the hard shoulder to avoid a traffic jam; driving the wrong way down a divided highway so as to effect a shortcut; or veering suddenly across three lanes of traffic with only a languid hand flapped out of the window in lieu of a signal.

Fares are regulated by "stages" and payment is made to the "tout" who operates the sliding door. Those in the know suggest that it is best to sit at the back, and never in the "death seat," which is by the driver. As a general rule of thumb, hang on to your valuables, don't use your cell phone unless you have to, and if the locals look nervous either politely ask the driver to slow down, or ask to get off. Traveling at night is not recommended due to hazards ranging from potholes, poor street lighting, a relaxed attitude toward operational headlights, and armed holdups.

Private Bus Services
There are privately operated intercity bus services between the major towns and cities. It is advisable to book in advance, but not essential. Refer to the "Bus Companies" section in the telephone directory's

Yellow Pages. There is also a daily shuttle service running between Nairobi and Arusha, Tanzania.

Taxis

There are plenty of taxi stands to be found outside the main hotels, shopping arcades, and central points in cities. Alternatively there are a number of dial-up taxi firms operating in the major towns. A tariff sheet should be available and it is wise to agree upon the price of the journey before you set off.

Car Rental

There are many well-established and reputable car rental companies in operation. To rent a car you must be over twenty-three and under seventy years and have held a driver's license for a minimum of two years. Prices vary enormously so shopping around is recommended, as is four-wheel drive. Kenyan motorists drive on the left and pass on the right. Road conditions in many places are difficult.

Hitching a Lift

Kenyans habitually hitch lifts—often the only way to get around in the less populated areas, other than by walking. While it is not suggested that visitors try this, giving a hitcher a lift is a great way to meet a cross section of Kenyans.

The correct way to hitch in Kenya is by waving the hand rapidly up and down with the palm facing downward (which can sometimes also indicate that you are willing to pay for the ride, but not always). Hitching by means of an upturned thumb is not recommended. This gesture can indicate your support for one of the major political parties.

Driving in Kenya

Kenyans drive on the left side of the road and, in general, European-style traffic rules and road markings apply. Visitors to Kenya are, however, often alarmed by Kenyan driving, which can be fast and apparently reckless.

Passing another vehicle is usually done at speed, often on a bend or on the brow of a hill, and with seeming indifference as to what might be coming in the opposite direction. To this end, Kenyan drivers make great use of their headlights, vigorously flashing those on the "wrong" side of the road (from their point of view). It is also customary to flash the right-hand signal to suggest that it is dangerous to pass, and the left-hand signal to suggest that it is safe to pass; the latter should not be taken literally and, in general, "defensive" driving is recommended. In the case of a breakdown, it is the Kenyan custom to strew broken tree branches on the road at some distance

before and after the vehicle to alert oncoming traffic to the danger; and should the driver require assistance he or she will flag down a fellow driver by waving a hand up and down.

SECURITY TIPS

Never leave valuables in your car.

Always lock your car.

Always padlock spare wheels.

Always roll your windows up at urban traffic lights.

Traffic Charity

In built-up areas you will often find that you are petitioned by beggars when you stop at the traffic lights. Invariably polite, usually severely disabled, and spending long hours in the hot sun, they are hard to refuse. Visitors should, however, beware of gangs of "street children" who also petition drivers at traffic lights. Tragic though their circumstances are, the fact remains that giving them money encourages more children to be abandoned to the streets. It also encourages glue sniffing, a habit to which many street children are addicted.

Traffic Retailing

Wherever there is a traffic jam in Kenya, there will be a troop of street vendors selling everything from magazines to "designer" sunglasses. Should you wish to buy, bargaining is expected; and if the traffic moves on before you have completed your purchase the vendor will catch up with you. Depend upon it.

Bogus Bling

The tale is told, apocryphal or not, of Maasai warriors around the Ngorongoro Crater in Tanzania who were regularly given expensive designer watches by compassionate, and wealthy, American tourists. Having no use for such items, the warriors sold them on, usually to other white people, on the roadside. Soon the word got round that you could get "a genuine Rolex for peanuts" at a certain spot, and the locals flocked to buy them. Subsequently, the Maasai ran out of genuine Rolexes and, reluctant to lose the income, traveled to the big cities to buy fakes. Business resumed.

Kenyan Police Road Blocks

A length of iron chain fitted with large spikes, extending across the road from either side allowing a small gap in the middle, and often preceded by a warning triangle (sometimes reading "Accident Ahead") indicates a roadblock by the Kenyan police. If the officers require you to stop they will point directly at you and wave you to the side of the road. Generally scrupulously polite and charming to visitors, a police officer may ask to see your driver's license, road tax, and proof of insurance before waving you on.

If, however, you have broken any of the rules of the road, this will be pointed out to you. Usually some thanks for the advice, a polite apology, and the promise not to transgress again will suffice but, should the police decide to charge you, you will be required to visit a police station and/or appear in court.

It is worth remembering during any exchange with the police that, like all Kenyans, they place great emphasis on politeness and are nearly always blessed with a good sense of humor.

Road Accidents
Visitors are advised against stopping at the scene of a serious accident, unless this is unavoidable, since feelings can run high when people have been injured, and blame (sometimes turning violent) can be wrongly apportioned.

Cycling
The Kenyan love their bicycles, often equipping them with customized padded saddles, decorations, and slogans on the mud flaps; only occasionally, however, do they equip them with lights, which makes driving at night a hazardous experience for cyclists and motorists alike. Kenyan cyclists also pride themselves on their ability to transport virtually anything on the back of a bike; loads can include goats, improbable piles of eggs in flimsy boxes, or "sofa sets." Small Kenyan boys, meanwhile, are often to be found balanced on the pedals of very large bikes, while their older brothers can be seen transporting their impeccably dressed girlfriends around—perched sidesaddle on a padded seat over the rear wheel. In Kisumu and around Lake Victoria *boda bodas* (bicycle taxis) are very popular; and during the rush hour it is common to see a besuited businessman reading his newspaper or operating his cell phone while perched elegantly on the back of a *boda boda*.

Several guidebooks suggest that it is fine for visitors to cycle in Kenya and that in this manner

they can "get to parts of the country that would be hard to visit by any other means." This is, however, not recommended, partly because of the poor roads, vicious potholes, high altitude, and often searing heat, but mainly because Kenyan drivers are not noted for their respect for cyclists. The same goes for motorcycling.

Walking
Walking is a way of life for the average Kenyan: schoolchildren walk for up to three hours to get to school, many Kenyans walk long distances to work, and going for an evening or Sunday stroll is a regular pastime and method of courtship. It isn't easy for a visitor to walk in Kenya, though, especially in the towns, where sidewalks are a rarity and muggings are frequent, or in the rural areas, where the roadside is largely the preserve of cows, goats, and cyclists.

There's also the fact that Kenyans don't expect to see white people walking: the local whites never do.

This can result in a walker being stared at or becoming the target of unwelcome attention.

Walking around Nairobi after dusk is not recommended (due to frequent muggings); nor is venturing into non-tourist areas on foot at any time. The general rule if you wish to walk is to walk briskly and with purpose, to decline politely offers to "show you around," and never to wear or otherwise display any items of value.

WHERE TO STAY

One of Africa's prime tourist destinations, and the longest established, Kenya's tourist infrastructure is tried and tested. The range of accommodation is comprehensive, and few people in the world are as welcoming as the Kenyans.

Hotels

Hotels vary enormously in price and facilities, and the one- to five-star rating given by the Ministry of

Tourism is not an accurate basis of comparison. Better
to inquire at a local travel agent or book through one
of the larger hotel chains. Kenya's luxury hotels offer
excellent standards of service and are comparable
to the best hotels anywhere in the world. First- and
second-class hotels vary widely in service and facilities
but are generally comfortable, with private bathrooms
and European-style food. Small rural hotels (*hoteli*)
will offer extremely basic accommodation and are
not recommended to visitors for a number of reasons
ranging from security to hygiene.

Lodges
Lodges are located in the national parks and reserves
and are, of necessity, limited; they are also usually
expensive. The food and facilities, however, are
generally of the highest standard.

Tented Camps
Comprising a small selection of permanently sited
canvas tents, which are roofed, pitched on a concrete

base or raised wooden platform, and often with a bathroom to the rear, tented camps have little to do with the vacations under canvas that visitors might have experienced. Most offer a surprising degree of luxury, with flush toilets, hot and cold running water, and electricity.

Self-catering Accommodation
Economically priced self-catering *bandas* (simple chalets) are available in many game parks and range from simple *rondavels* to the houses that the wardens used to live in. Usually delightfully situated, they offer cooking facilities (which can range from a propane gas stove to a campfire) and varying standards of bed/bath facilities.

A wide range of privately owned self-catering villas, houses, and beach cottages are also available.

Private Home Stays
These offer the chance of staying in a, usually white, Kenyan household, many of which are colonial-style farms in beautiful settings. The downside (for some) is that you will probably be expected to eat with your hosts, who may or may not regale you with safari tales. Prices vary greatly.

Campsites
There are more than two hundred official campsites in wilderness areas throughout the country, many in the national parks. Facilities vary. "Special Campsites" are booked exclusively in advance; otherwise you pay as you go. Beware: leaving your camp unattended is not recommended, not least because the baboons have learned to operate zippers.

HEALTH AND SAFETY

Travelers should take out adequate medical insurance. A number of vaccinations are recommended—check these in advance.

Malaria

Malaria is endemic in tropical Africa and protection against it is absolutely necessary. It is recommended that a reliable prophylactic medicine be taken for two weeks before arrival, all the time while in the country, and for four to six weeks after returning home. In mosquito-ridden areas sleep under mosquito nets, cover your arms and legs in the evening, and use an insect repellent.

Snake Bites

Of the 126 species of snakes found in Kenya, ninety-three are neither venomous nor dangerous and over half of the bites inflicted are "dry" (not envenomed), either because the snake intended the bite as a warning, or because it was low on venom. However, prevention is better than cure so, when walking in the bush, follow the instructions of your guide: wear boots, socks, and pants; avoid walking in long grass; and look where you are putting your feet.

If you are bitten do not panic: immobilize the bitten limb with a rough splint, and apply a bandage to the bite. Do not apply a tourniquet, do not cut either side of the bite, and do not suck the bite. Get medical help as soon as possible.

HIV/AIDS

HIV/AIDS is a serious problem in Africa: around 5 percent of Kenya's population are HIV positive.

Medical Services

There are plenty of highly qualified doctors, surgeons, and dentists in both Nairobi and Mombasa. Nairobi has five modern and well-equipped hospitals, Mombasa two. In addition, lodges and hotels in the remoter game reserves usually have resident medical staff. Most lodges also have radio or telephone contact with the Flying Doctor Service in Nairobi.

Personal Safety

Great efforts have been made by the Kenyan government to improve security. However, since Kenyan society is less affluent than that of the developed world, ostentatious or careless displays of wealth or valuables will attract thieves. It is best to leave all valuables in the hotel safe, wear no jewelry, and carry no expensive items of technology. It is wise also to walk briskly, and politely but firmly to decline all inappropriate offers of friendship, guiding, or any other interaction: sadly, the majority will be suspect.

Visitors are also advised to think twice before shouting "thief" in the case of a street mugging in an urban area. In such instances it is not unknown for citizens to attempt to stone, lynch, or otherwise attack those caught "red-handed," often resulting in the death of the perceived perpetrator. Visitors are also advised against stopping at the scene of a serious road accident, since their well-meaning attempts to help can often be wrongly construed by an angry and emotionally charged group of bystanders.

chapter eight

BUSINESS BRIEFING

THE BUSINESS CULTURE

The conduct of business is similar to that in the West. Most negotiations are carried out in the "official" language of English, and the legal system is loosely based on that established by the British. Key differences do exist, however, all of which reflect specifically Kenyan values and attitudes. There are also geographical differences: in Nairobi the pace of business is fast; in coastal Mombasa the sheer heat and humidity means that everyone proceeds at a slower pace; and "up country" (north of Nairobi) business life generally moves to a more sedate rhythm. By and large, Kenyan business culture is formal and conservative. Businesspeople are smartly presented and, in general, if you want to be taken seriously you should wear a suit and present a business card.

Buzzwords and Jargon

Kenyan businesspeople are fascinated by buzzwords, jargon, and business fashions. "Mission statements" are a must; "branding" took the business community by storm, shortly after followed by "re-branding." "Stakeholders," at one stage, appeared in just about every proposal, and words such as "facilitate," "sensitize," and "modality" all enjoyed a brief reign: some still do. Sometimes the overuse of complicated terminology (not all of which is fully understood by those who employ it), and the incidence of "why use one word when you can use ten?" syndrome makes the business culture seem cumbersome, but this is often offset by the enthusiasm and ready humor of the participants.

Corporate Social Responsibility

One of the latest "fashions" to hit the Kenyan business scene revolves around the need to demonstrate "Corporate Social Responsibility" (CRS). This can take many forms: contributions to the community, support of health initiatives, ecological projects, or even the promotion of Kenyan culture. Any contributions that the visiting businessperson can make to the CSR effort of the company with which he or she is dealing will, therefore, be much appreciated.

THE BUSINESS COMMUNITY

Kenya's business world is broadly divided: first, into the urban and informal business communities; and second, into those businesses that are run by the Asian community (usually an entirely Asian management team and an entirely Kenyan workforce), those that

are run by the black Kenyan community (in which both management and workers are black Kenyan, though in some cases the accounting staff may be Asian), and the few businesses that continue to retain a CEO, and sometimes sales, marketing, and administration executives, who are white (such as the leading banks, some sectors of the travel industry, and most of the large-scale horticultural sector).

The Urban Business Community

Fast moving and dynamic, the urban business community bristles with well-educated, articulate people, all of whom are highly computer literate. Gone are the days when whites headed most of the major companies; nowadays most of Kenya's CEOs are Kenyan.

The Informal Business Sector

There is a booming informal sector of small-scale traders, craftspeople, and entrepreneurs. Many small traders operate from roadside *kiosks* (small wooden sheds), others from single rooms in custom-built trading blocks. A large percentage are known as "*Jua Kali*" ("in the hot sun") because they work by the roadside, sometimes with shelter, sometimes not. Supremely adaptable, whatever you want made, copied, or created, the Kenyan informal business sector can provide it—and fast. One Nairobi-based furniture designer reckoned that it took approximately eight hours for her latest designs to be noted, copied, and available for sale by the side of the road.

The Kenyan Labor Force

Kenya's labor force numbers 18.21 million (2015 est.), the vast majority of whom work outside the formal sector, either as subsistence farmers and herders or in the urban informal sector. The unemployment rate was approximately 40 percent in 2015. The majority of corporate employees enjoy union representation, most of which is divided by industry sector. Strikes are rare due to the paucity of employment and the fact that each salary supports a large extended family.

Women in Business

Kenyan women make astute and ruthless entrepreneurs, and many positions of authority are occupied by women. Hardworking, ambitious, and shrewd, they are adept at multitasking and seem to juggle family, husbands, and home life with ease.

It used to be the case that lower down the business hierarchy, sexual favors had to be granted by women in order to rise up the ladder (or even to get a job in the first place), but this is increasingly frowned upon.

MAKING CONTACT

Personal contacts and introductions count, and personal references are highly respected. There are several powerful business networks, the most noteworthy being the multiracial Rotarians, who have branches in all major cities. Other "clubs" include the private member clubs (such as the Muthaiga Club and the Nairobi Club, though perversely neither allows "business" to be conspicuously conducted on the premises), a broad range of Asian associations, and the golf clubs. The trade associations governing the various industrial sectors (the flower industry, for instance, is governed by the Flower Council), can all prove invaluable to the visiting businessperson.

Appointments should ideally be made at least two weeks in advance, and it is imperative that they be reconfirmed two or three days before the meeting. It is also wise, before setting off for a meeting, just to check that it is still on. Things change, problems occur, key decision makers can be suddenly called away.

"FLEXITIME"

As in other areas of Kenyan life, business operates according to "Swahili Time," which is not quite as exact as visitors from Europe or America may expect. It is generally understood that if a meeting is to begin at, for instance, 8:30 a.m., it may well not get properly started until 9:30. By the same token, if you are late for a business event in Kenya, nobody gets unduly irritated, especially not if you signal your punctuality problems in advance.

MEETINGS

Kenyan business revolves around "the meeting," which is usually a formal affair. Meetings are often lengthy due to the egalitarian nature of the Kenyan people, and to their insistence that not only should everyone get their say, but also that every remark, criticism, or suggestion should be given careful consideration. Attempts to rush a meeting will generally simply lengthen it. Seating is usually hierarchical and meetings often begin with everyone standing up and introducing themselves. Eye contact is imperative, and plentiful handshakes the norm.

Large meetings are usually punctuated by a coffee break; small meetings include the offer of tea or coffee. (Neither of these conforms to Western expectations: if in doubt ask for water and don't be surprised if you are asked "hot or cold?" Kenyans like to drink hot water.) These days it is customary to turn off your cell phone when entering a meeting.

Kenyans like to begin and end proceedings by shaking hands, exchanging cards (business cards have often "run out" so be prepared with paper and pen), and exchanging small talk. Invariably polite, they always listen carefully to what the visitor has to say, and would think it very rude to interrupt, curtail, contradict, or generally cause the visitor to lose "face." Visitors should accord their Kenyan hosts similar respect.

Presentations

If invited to make a presentation, you can expect to address a sizable group, not all of whom you will have met before. Presentations are formal

affairs, so the use of audiovisual aids is highly recommended, informational handouts/statistics are welcomed, and "question time" is a must.

Decision Making

Gregarious and egalitarian, most Kenyans prefer to reach group decisions, and are often loath to stand up and be counted, preferring to stay within the safety of the collective. Finding the ultimate decision maker (or the person who signs the checks) can also prove time-consuming, but rest assured, he or she will unquestionably emerge as negotiations progress. As to whether a "hard sell" works, in general it does not, for a number of reasons: the Kenyans are very curious and like to examine things from all angles; they are wary and astute bargainers and traders; group decisions are preferred (and all the members are rarely present); and, finally, politeness is paramount.

CONTRACTS

It is recommended that visitors engage local accountants and lawyers (also known as advocates) to work on contract issues. They will understand the intricacies of the Kenyan legal and accountancy systems, the possible pitfalls, and the best solutions to problems that arise. Nothing involving paperwork and signatures ever happens quickly; changes and amendments are normal.

Many large Kenyan contracts are awarded by tender. Tenders are usually advertised in both daily papers; applications must be submitted exactly by the deadline with all supporting documentation (to avoid disqualification), and are judged according to a list of merits known only to the evaluation committee.

GETTING THINGS DONE

There may sometimes appear to be a gap between what people say can, may, or will happen in business, and what actually does happen. This has a lot to do with the fact that the Kenyans don't like to say "No," or give a negative reaction, much preferring to say "Yes," or "no problem." It is also related to the greater impact of speech than the written word. Diligent follow-up and phone calls are imperative, as is the noting down and circulation of who is supposed to be doing what.

Nor should visiting business folk be surprised if what was supposed to happen has not happened by the appointed time. Although Kenyans are proficient in delegation and each person's area of responsibility is clearly defined, problems occur when a key person (and "key" can include seemingly lowly members of the organization, such as the secretary) is absent (due to family problems, ill health, sudden taking of "leave," or numerous other unpredictable situations), as other members of the team may be reluctant to assume responsibility for the work.

Humor

Finally, if things don't go to plan, patience, humor, and gentle pushing generally succeed where displays of anger or impatience do not. As in other areas of life in Kenya, the use of humor, banter, and mild jokes is appreciated and helps to break the ice. Kenyans love being made to laugh, and to make others laugh.

Working with Kenyans

Because they are a welcoming, relaxed people who delight in humor and in getting to know people, working alongside Kenyans is invariably a pleasure. Problems can occur due to their relaxed attitude toward punctuality, brevity, and delivery of what is required, but all can be overcome with patience and an appreciation of the problems and restrictions with which they work.

Keeping in Touch

Most business relationships take time to develop and keeping in touch is imperative. The Kenyans are very fond of saying "You were lost!" in tones of incredulity, if regular contact is not maintained. How to keep in touch depends on the industry, but letters, e-mails, phone calls, even text messages, work equally well.

BUSINESS ENTERTAINING

Breakfast, lunch, and dinner meetings are all acceptable forms of business entertaining and vary greatly. Sometimes wives or partners are invited, sometimes not. Sometimes, seemingly unconnected friends or relations will turn up with the Kenyan business contact, with no explanation given; this relates to the complicated web of social obligations and arrangements within Kenyan society, and should be accepted with good grace.

In both Mombasa and Nairobi the Asian business community either goes home for lunch, or brings lunch from home. Many Asian businesspeople are teetotalers and vegetarian, which should be taken into account when offering entertainment. In Mombasa everyone takes a lengthy lunch break (to avoid the heat), while in Nairobi the fast-moving management echelons increasingly snatch a quick lunch, or go without.

Finally, as we have seen, Kenyans like to eat and take it seriously—keep business talk brief, and for the end of the meal—and punctuality is rare. A lot of useful networking is done on the golf course.

ADVERTISING AND PROMOTION

Kenya has a thriving advertising and PR industry. All companies of any size have a Web site, and many provide corporate promotional CDs or DVDs. It is also worth noting that just about every company provides a free calendar in the New Year, and that these are immensely popular (a great introductory medium for visiting businesses). Other welcome business gifts include diaries, pens, and desk sets. Lower down the business hierarchy the promotional T-shirt or baseball cap are always energetically sought after.

NEPOTISM AND TRIBALISM

Thanks to the nature of Kenyan society, the predominance of elaborate extended families, and the belief that "family comes first," it can be that jobs, contracts, or general preference are extended on a "who you are" or "who you know" basis, rather than on competence. Until lately, this attitude also took into consideration "what tribe" you came from. More recently, however, such behavior has been disapproved of.

CORRUPTION AND GRAFT

Though the government is making strenuous efforts to eradicate corruption, the concept of "one favor deserves another" still holds sway. Increasingly, however, businesses and parastatals are encouraging people to expose corruption. When faced with the suggestion that "something small" would help grease the wheels the visitor has a number of options: ignore the suggestion, genially fail to understand it, or go along with it in an oblique manner ("give" something for an alternative reason, say, for a beer).

FINDING WORK IN KENYA AS A VISITOR

In order to work in Kenya, visitors require a work permit (divided into various categories depending upon whether one is a "consultant" or an employee). Work permits are linked to immigration status, can be difficult to obtain, are generally renewable every two years, and are stamped into your passport. In order to get a permit, you must satisfy the authorities as to your tax status by presenting audited accounts, and a tax PIN number is now obligatory.

chapter nine

COMMUNICATING

LANGUAGE

In Kenya the "official" language is English, the
"national" language is Kiswahili, and there are
multiple ethnic languages. Eighty-seven percent of
the population over the age of fifteen are literate.
Increasingly, those involved in tourism also have a
smattering of Italian, German, and French.

Most people in Kenya speak Swahili with varying
degrees of purity. The term Swahili derives from the
Arab word *sahel,* meaning coast, and the language
came into being 1,300 years ago when Arab and
Persian traders settled on the East African coast. Since
then it has spread to become the *lingua franca* of East
Africa. Basically a Bantu language, modern Swahili has
incorporated thousands of foreign words, the majority
Arabic.

Speaking English in Kenya

Since most Kenyans are bilingual (tribal
language and Swahili), if not trilingual
(tribal language, Swahili, and English),
and since English is not always their
first language, there may initially be
communication difficulties. This is
not necessarily because of a Kenyan

weakness in English, but more often because Kenyan English and "English/American" English are different.

Intonation can vary, stresses tend to be put on different words, seemingly antiquated words are used, such as "I alighted at the bus stop" rather than "I got off the bus," and quirky phrases occur. For instance, a Kenyan may not go to "pick something up;" he or she goes to "pick" it. "You know" is widely used, either at the beginning or the end of a sentence; "even" and "in fact" crop up in unexpected places; "he" and "she" get mixed up; and if you've been out of touch you'll be accused of "being lost!" Conversation is liberally strewn with Swahili words and phrases, of which the most common are: *jambo* (hello), *karibu* (welcome), *kwaheri* (good-bye), *asante* (thank you), *hakuna matata* (no problem), and *pole pole* (slowly, slowly).

From the Kenyan point of view, most visitors speak too quickly, so if in doubt speak slowly and clearly until your listener has got his or her "ear" attuned. This is specially relevant when speaking on the phone—when spelling out names, giving directions, or giving phone numbers, always say "Would you like to read that back to me?"

PROPER ACKNOWLEDGMENT

Eye contact is important. In Kenya it is customary to *see* your fellow man and acknowledge him or her with a smile, a gesture (a raised hand, or the raising of both hands, which indicates peace), or a greeting (*jambo),* rather than to look straight through them, as often happens in the larger cities of the West. Kenyans also often address each other by their surnames, and may do likewise to visitors. This indicates friendly familiarity.

FORMS OF ADDRESS
Traditional
When talking to a man, the polite form of address is *Bwana*, which is a combination of Mister and Sir. For anybody clearly over forty the term *Mezee* (old man, elder) is considered polite, expressing respect for the person and his wisdom and experience; it is often used in deference to gray hair. For women the word *Mama* carries the same connotation, but is used for women of all ages (with or without children). Children are addressed as *watoto* (singular *toto*). People whose name you don't know but whose attention you want to attract can be addressed as *Rafiki* (friend), *Bwana,* or *Mama.*

Modern Youth
The youth of Kenya have evolved a language called "Sheng," the equivalent of French *argot* or British slang. A mix of Swahili and countless other things, it will probably remain a closed book to you. The influence of TV and films, however, can be recognized in the use of terms such as "girlfriend" or "my dear" among friendly females, and "brother" or "friend" among bonding males. "You guys" and "you people" are also used.

TOPICS OF CONVERSATION
Kenyans love talking and few topics are taboo. If in doubt visitors can always inquire how the weather has been, or whether there has been any rain—the arrival or departure of the rains is a national obsession, since so many people depend upon them for their

crops. Among men, sport is always a welcome topic, especially soccer, while among women the usual suspects apply: fashion, relationships, children, homes, food, and so forth. Discussion of Kenyan politics is always popular, though make sure you are well-informed.

Swearing is not considered polite among men and is unheard of among women. Blasphemy is highly offensive.

HUMOR

Kenyans delight in laughter, adore long and convoluted "shaggy dog" stories, revel in jokes, and are generally eager to see the funny side of things. If you are pulled over by the police, give them a smile, crack a joke, and nine times out of ten they will beam broadly and let you go. When confronted with the solemn face of bureaucracy, a well-placed smile will often speed things along, while waiters and waitresses love to be amused by tales of your day (taking it as a personal and national accolade that you have enjoyed yourself). Kenyans are great raconteurs and excellent listeners; you will often find people who live, work, and eat together every day enthusiastically regaling each other with stories.

SHAKING HANDS AND KISSING CHEEKS

A generally tactile people, who often reach out to touch during conversation, Kenyans shake hands all the time and at every occasion; indeed it would be considered most impolite on meeting someone not to shake hands, regardless of whether you had met them earlier or had never seen them before in your life. Sometimes both hands are used, sometimes a special handshake is used, involving clasped thumbs, sometimes a very languid handshake is proffered (among women), while if hands are wet or dirty an elbow or forearm is presented for shaking in lieu. Should you say something particularly funny or apposite during a conversation, you may also find a hand put up for the Kenyan equivalent of a "high five." You may also notice that if you meet someone you have not seen for some time, they may hold on to your hand long after the shaking is finished in a general demonstration of how pleased they are to see you.

The "air kissing" of cheeks between women; and between women and men who know each other well, is becoming increasingly common in urban Kenya, though, like anywhere else in the world other than France, nobody is quite sure whether to lunge first to the right or to the left.

BODY LANGUAGE AND GESTURES

Kenyan men are often seen holding hands, which has nothing to do with sexual orientation and everything to do with fellowship. A shadow from the colonial days, pointing with your finger at someone is considered very rude, as is summoning with a crooked finger or beckoning with the palm up (beckon with the palm down). Finally, and in deference to the Arabic influence of the Swahili peoples, the left hand is traditionally reserved for unhygienic acts, and the right hand for eating and touching or passing things.

THE MEDIA

The Kenyan media is a potent force. Once hampered by government strictures, it now enjoys almost complete freedom. Newspapers are read avidly and may pass through many hands, locally produced magazines are increasingly popular (imported "glossies" are available but expensive), just about everyone has a radio (the lifeline of rural areas), and television is hugely popular.

The Kenya Broadcasting Corporation (KBC) has radio transmission in English, Swahili, Hindi, and African languages. The BBC World Service (which also transmits on 93.7 FM), Voice of America, and Deutsche Welle all transmit on short-wave frequencies. Commercial radio stations include Capital FM and Kiss FM.

There are locally produced television channels in English and Swahili, but program choice is limited. South Africa based digital satellite TV with a large selection of channels has become popular with the mid to high income groups.

There are two English-language newspapers, the *Daily Nation* and the *Standard*, and two Swahili newspapers, *Taifa Leo* and *Kenya Leo*.

KEEPING IN TOUCH
Mail
The Kenyan postal system is run by Posta, the government Postal Corporation of Kenya. Outgoing letters rarely go astray (but can take up to two weeks to reach Australia or the USA), while incoming letters can take four to seven days to reach their destination.

The "Messenger"
Due to the fact that the Kenyan postal system uses POBs (numbered Post Office Boxes), if you want something to arrive at its destination fast, it's best to deliver it by hand. Thus most businesses employ "messengers," who use either motorcycles (in Swahili, *picky-picky*) or public transportation to dash around the urban centers with letters, contracts, checks, and the like.

Word of Mouth
A legacy of the nomadic tradition, the Kenyan "grapevine" is extraordinarily efficient. Kenyans can transmit news or messages without the use of post or telecommunications, with unerring speed and accuracy, over huge distances. The system works on the basis of close cooperation, and the transmitted knowledge of who's where, who's traveling, who knows who, and more.

Internet, E-mail, and Wi-Fi
As with most things technical, the urban Kenyans have taken to the Internet with gusto (Internet users in 2015:

16.5 million). Most young professionals have an e-mail address, most businesses have a Web site, and most towns have at least one Internet café. There is Internet access in nearly all the main post offices in the country. Many of the luxury hotels also offer data ports in the rooms and Wi-Fi hotspots.

Telephones
The Kenyan fixed or landline phone system is run by the state organization Telkom Kenya, which in the past was renowned for its inefficiency. Lines were habitually disconnected without notice or reason, reconnection involved weeks of pleading, clarity was poor, and the cost of phone calls (especially international) high.

Recently, and thanks to the competition presented by the cell phone revolution, there has been considerable improvement and innovation: "customer service," a concept hitherto unknown, has been introduced, technical service has improved, and costs have been brought down. However, the service is still unreliable, lines are poor, and instances of "echo"

(hearing your own voice) are common, and irritating.
Telkom prepaid phone cards, allowing pay-as-you-go
calls on any landline, are also available, as is VOIP
(voice over internet protocol) access.

PHONE ESSENTIALS

International telephone code +254

To dial out of the country, dial 000 followed
by the required country code.

The Cell Phone Revolution

Cell phones, also known as "mobiles" in Kenya,
are immensely popular, not least because of the
inadequacies of the fixed line system. According to
the *Daily Nation*, there were nearly 38 million cell
phone users in Kenya in 2016, and it is estimated that
80 percent of all calls are made by cell phone.
Initially, call rates were high, but they have come
down considerably. Most subscribers use the prepaid
service—pay-as-you-go with scratch cards that can
be purchased just about anywhere and in affordable
denominations. A postpaid service is also available.

Kenya uses the GSM 900 system, which is compatible
with Europe and Australia but not North America.
Handsets are easily and cheaply available, as are SIM
cards (sold in a prepaid starter pack from the main
providers Safaricom and Airtel). Coverage is good, other
than in far-flung rural areas and in some of the national
parks and reserves.

The advent of the cell phone has brought about a
revolution in communications in Kenya. Previously,
only the affluent could afford a phone; now just about
every city dweller has a cell phone, while in the rural
areas small *kiosks* provide the use of a cell phone for
a fee, and take incoming calls. The cell phone has
transformed business in the private sector, especially in
agricultural areas where producers can now cut out the
middleman and do business direct.

The arrival of the cell phone has also changed social
behavior: families living "up country" can be contacted
by those working in the urban areas; husbands are
expected to call home if they are going to be late,
adolescents can flag their movements to their parents,
and social arrangements are quickly and easily made.

Texting
Anyone with a cell phone in Kenya will almost
certainly be obsessed with texting, which is both
efficient and economical. All over the country you see
wrinkled brows as users painstakingly punch out their
messages—just about everyone is supremely "text-lit,"
and texting is an accepted form of conducting business.

Buzzing
Particularly at the end of the month when money is
short, or if the user has run out of prepaid usage on

his or her phone, they will "buzz" you by calling your number then immediately disconnecting. When this happens, you are expected to call them back.

Where and When to Use Your Cell Phone
As in the West, many public institutions now ban the use of cell phones. Some even levy fines on those who disregard the notices, notably in private clubs. Using a cell phone (unless you have hands-free equipment) when you are driving is illegal and will result in being pulled over by the police. Showing a cell phone on the street or in other crowded areas is unwise, since there is a booming trade in snatched phones, and an industry devoted to unlocking them.

CONCLUSION
Kenya is a land of ancient lineage and enormous contrasts, both of which are reflected in the colorful kaleidoscope of her people, whose patience, acceptance, warmth, humor, and hospitality invariably make a lasting impression upon the visitor. Few leave the country untouched or unmoved by their interaction with the Kenyan people; most leave with an enlightened spirit, and an ardent desire to return. We hope that this book has helped to explain something of the  dynamics of Kenyan society, and will lead to a happy and lasting cultural exchange.

Further Reading

Peoples and Cultures of Kenya

Fedders, Andrew, Cynthia Salvadori, *Peoples and Cultures of Kenya*. London and Nairobi: Transafrica Nairobi and Rex Collins, in association with KTDC, 1981.

Foottit, Claire, *Kenya. The Bradt Travel Guide*. Chalfont St Giles, UK and Guilford, Conn.: Bradt Travel Guides and The Globe Pequot Press, 2004.

Kenyatta, Jomo. *Facing Mount Kenya*. London and Nairobi : Vintage and Heinemann Kenya, 1979.

Kenya and Africa

Huxley, Elspeth. *Nine Faces of Kenya*. London: Harvill, imprint of HarperCollins, 1990.

Markham, Beryl. *West with the Night*. London: Virago, 1989.

Miller, Charles. *The Lunatic Express*. London: Macdonald, 1972; Penguin, 2001.

Naipaul, Shiva. *North of South*. Harmondsworth: Penguin, 1980.

Ngugi wa Thiong'o. *A Grain of Wheat*. London: Penguin, 2002.

Pakenham, Thomas. *The Scramble for Africa, 1879–1912*. London: Abacus, 1992.

Reader, John. *Africa: A Biography of the Continent*. London: Penguin, 1997.

Wainaina, Binyavana. *Discovering Home*. Johannesburg: Jacana Media, 2003.

Tourist Information

Kenya Tourist Board

For details on travel, accommodation, and tourism options:

Tel.: +254 (0)20 2711262

E-mail: info@kenyatourism.org, www.magicalkenya.com

Safety and Communication Centre of the Kenya Tourism Federation

For up-to-the minute safety and security advice:

Tel.: +254 (0)20 604767, 604729

Cell phone: 0733 617499 or 0722 745645

24-hour tourist helpline: tel.: +254 (0)20 604767/605485

Kenya Wildlife Service (KWS)

For information on the Kenyan National Parks and Reserves:

Tel.: + 254 (0) 20 600800

E-mail: tourism@kws.org or www.kws.org

culture smart! kenya

Index